SAS
& OTHER SPECIAL
FORCES

HarperCollins*Publishers*

Text by Ernest Wood

HarperCollins*Publishers*
PO Box, Glasgow G4 0NB

First Published 1996
© HarperCollins*Publishers* 1996

3 5 7 9 10 8 6 4 2

ISBN 0 00 470991 8

Printed in Italy by Amadeus S.p.A.,Rome

Contents

Introduction

The United States Department of Defense Dictionary of Military Terms defines special forces as "Military personnel with cross training in basic and specialised military skills, organised into small, multi-purpose detachments with the mission to train, organise, supply, direct, and control indigenous forces in guerrilla warfare and counter-insurgency operations and to conduct unconventional warfare operations".

Special forces have however existed since the beginnings of organised war. In 1100BC Gideon initiated a guerrilla and conventional campaign

Special Forces in training: wearing a gas mask, body armour and fire-resistant uniform, they prepare to assault a building from the roof.

At the close of the war in Rhodesia a group of Patriotic Front guerrillas arrive at an assembly point. The ZIPRA and ZANLA guerillas were armed and equipped by China and the Soviet Union.

against the Midianites and Amalakites, an Arabic people living east of the Jordan. The Old Testament (Judges 7) describes how Gideon initiated the first recorded 'selection process' to hone down his force into a flexible and motivated team. First he sent home all those who were frightened, reducing numbers from 22,000 to 10,000. After a tough march the remaining 10,000 reached a stream. Most of them 'switched off' and lay face down lapping up the water; only 300 remained alert, stooping to drink water by the handful. Gideon took this small group, split it into three and — using the advantage of night and shock psychological tactics — attacked the Amalakites and Midianites as they camped in a valley.

Gideon is a classic example of a charismatic leader selecting a small force and employing it with novel tactics to destroy a larger, less flexible one.

The real value of special forces was revealed after the Industrial Revolution. This produced a society which

Special Forces use many non-standard weapons. This M16A2 modified to function as a light machine gun was developed by the manufacturers for US Special Forces.

Small, handy, and firing a round designed to penetrate body armour, the Russian PSM pistol was first issued to the Soviet Spetsnaz units.

was no longer semi-rural and self-sufficient, but dependent on the free movement of goods and services by road, canal, rail, sea and finally air. The power to produce goods and move them came from water, steam power, electricity, the internal combustion engine and, later, nuclear energy. The fuel and power for this network had to be stored or distributed. Society had become a complex self-supporting structure which was vulnerable to attack.

So too as armies became equipment-heavy they

required fuel, ammunition and food, and developed long, vulnerable logistic trains. Though weapons were becoming more accurate and destructive, they were also becoming complex and vulnerable. They could be immobilised if fuel or spare parts were unavailable.

Tactical and strategic air attacks could be launched in depth against these military and civilian networks. But long before bombers had been built and flown, special forces — which could be landed by sea or inserted overland — had delivered precise attacks.

The Confederate cavalry raids of the American Civil

The Russian army has always believed in the value of snipers. The sniper's hood is see-through, and he is armed with an SVD 7.62 mm sniper rifle.

Detail of the SVD sniper rifle. This robust and reliable weapon is still in Russian service and has been widely exported

War hit Union depots, telegraph lines and railways. These were copied by the Boer Commandos forty years later in South Africa. About 17 years on, TE Lawrence built up a relationship with Hussein Sherif of Mecca and his son Feisal, which led to the Arab Revolt against the Turks. Interestingly the Revolt in the Desert marks a watershed in special forces operations, since they were conducted using aircraft, armoured vehicles, horses and camels as well as knives and automatic weapons. On the Western Front in

France, German Storm Troops employed infiltration by small groups to penetrate and disrupt the allied front.

The first airborne forces were used by the Soviet Union against 'bandits' in the Caucuses between the wars (Conflicts in the Caucuses have returned to haunt Russia in the 1990s). In World War II the Germans used gliders to carry combat engineers to attack the Belgian fort of Eben Emael. The Allies developed their own forces and techniques including seaborne and air landed groups. The US Rangers and British Commandos, as well as national airborne forces, were established during the war and survived its conclusion.

North Africa had a porous front line between 1940 and 1942, which allowed long range vehicle patrols to move freely, and here various Allied groups operated. The Special Air Service (SAS) along with the Long Range Desert Group (LRDG) and Popski's Private Army (PPA) operated against German and Italian forces deep in enemy territory. PPA fought in Italy and the SAS throughout Europe and the Aegean.

Though the SAS was disbanded at the end of the

This Heckler and Koch sub-machine gun is fitted with a laser sight which places a red dot on the target. A flashlight is also attached, not only providing light but improving the balance of the weapon.

war, it was revived soon afterwards and has continued through a careful selection process to produce outstanding soldiers and leaders. The title and techniques have been adopted by the Belgian, Rhodesian, Australian and New Zealand armies, and copied by numerous armed forces throughout the world.

Post war operations by special forces have included Korea and Malaysia, Borneo, Vietnam, Cambodia and Laos, the Yemen, Oman, the Falklands, Iran, Afghanistan, Iraq and Somalia. Some of these have involved 'hearts and minds' operations in which teams have given local governments medical and farming assistance; others have been training missions to teach military skills to local soldiers. Finally, some have been reconnaissance missions or direct attacks on human or infrastructure targets.

Modern special forces may have an extensive range of sophisticated weapons, surveillance and communications equipment, but with it they need superior military skills and psychological and physical resources. These are vital since they may be required to work in small groups deep in enemy territory, where the climate may be as hostile as the forces they are operating against. Observation posts (OPs), which may be claustrophobic burrows in hedges or scrub, will have to be manned by day and night.

The interior of the Iranian Embassy after the SAS stormed it in 1980: an operation that made this secretive British unit a household name.

Cross-training within the patrol will mean that men have more than one specialisation — for example a medic may also be a signaller, or a demolitions expert may have specialised weapons skills. Though the name has been used in jest, it contains a great deal of truth: these men really are 'super soldiers'.

In the final years of the 20th Century the versatility of special forces will ensure that they have a role worldwide. Though cruise missiles and 1,000lb laser-

guided bombs may be capable of hitting targets as small as air conditioning vents, special forces can observe, evaluate, and act independently and with an exact level of violence. Over 3,000 years later the shock tactics of Gideon's 300 selected men are still as effective as they were in the darkness of that crowded enemy camp.

Left: The US Stinger surface to air missile (SAM), the Stinger was first used by the SAS in the Falklands in 1982 and has since seen action in Africa, Afghanistan and Central America. Its light weight makes it an ideal weapon for special forces.

The death of a Huey, hit by a Stinger.

15

CHAPTER 1

The Heroic Elite

Chapter 1: The Heroic Elite

Writing about 500BC in Imperial China, Sun Tzu
Wu produced a book of military aphorisms which
guided tactics and strategy in China for centuries and
were adopted by Mao Tse Tung in his military
writings in the 1940s. Centuries before the 'Boss' of a
special forces patrol called his team together to discuss
an upcoming operation in what the SAS call a
'Chinese Parliament', Sun Tzu had identified some of
the principles of leadership which motivate soldiers,
non commissioned officers (NCOs) and officers:

"The general who advances without coveting fame
and retreats without fearing disgrace, whose only
thought is to protect his country and do good service
for his sovereign, is the jewel of the kingdom.
"Regard your soldiers as your children, and they will
follow you wherever you may lead. Look on them as
your own beloved sons, and they will stand by you
even unto death".

The operations undertaken by special forces succeed
in part because they are well equipped and briefed,
but also because the men have been carefully tested
and selected and because they are led by men they
trust, and who trust them.
Military history is full of examples of gifted,
charismatic leaders who have attracted a small group

of men — and sometimes women — who have achieved successes against greater numbers through a mixture of guile, surprise, courage and fighting skill. These men and their leaders are an elite.

Leadership alone will not win battles; equipment and training are the other two sides of a tripod which ensures success. Even the most courageous and successful soldier in special forces started as a nervous recruit. It was the tough but intelligent training, combined with their own motivation, that made them 'special'. Superior equipment can include weapons, communications, transportation, and sensors and intelligence gathering equipment.

Biblical special forces

The Bible gives us a good example of special weapons, training, tactics and leadership with Joshua, Gideon and David. Gideon's selection course and novel tactics are covered in the introduction to this book. Before Gideon's operations, Joshua was leading the children of Israel from Egypt to occupy the Promised Land, "a land flowing with milk and honey". He sent "two spies" on a long range reconnaissance patrol to check the land. These unnamed operators penetrated Jericho and found a "safe house" belonging to Rahab, "a harlot". Rahab not only concealed them among drying flax on her roof, but facilitated their escape by rope over the city walls. She also struck a deal with them. When Jericho fell after a siege which included some ingenious 'psychological operations' it was "utterly destroyed... both man and woman, young and old, and ox and sheep and ass with the edge of the sword" in what would now be called ethnic cleansing, but Rahab and her family survived.

David's use of a sling to stun the massive Philistine warrior Goliath around 1010BC is an excellent example of technology and training. With time on his hands as a shepherd, the young David had developed his skill with a sling to the level that he could send a golf ball sized pebble accurately at a target area the size of a man's forehead. The sling might be new technology on the battlefield, but its effective use required a high level of training and skill.

The longbow – a technological advantage

Many centuries later King Henry V's defeat of the French at Agincourt is a fascinating example of the king as charismatic leader; his Welsh bowmen the skilled technicians of war, expert with their weapons. The French had already suffered defeat at Crecy in 1346, when an English force of 10,000 defeated 24,000 French and Genoese. The French losses were 11 princes, 1,200 knights and 8,000 others. At Poitiers ten years later 7,000 English under King

Edward and the charismatic Black Prince faced 18,000 French. By combining the shock effect of showers of arrows with a flank attack, the English routed the French — killing 8,000 and capturing the French King John II, who was ransomed for the massive sum of œ500,000.

In October 1415 a force of 9,000 tired and sick English and Welsh soldiers were confronted by a force of about 30,000 French under Constable d'Albert. The defensive position chosen by King Henry V funnelled the French heavy cavalry. The archers had also built a palisade of stakes which broke the charge of French men-at-arms. It was a harsh battle, with the Anglo Welsh force losing 130 and the French 5,000 killed, including the Constable and three dukes. A thousand prisoners were taken, including the Duke of Orleans and Marshal Jean Bouciqaut. When heavily armoured horses and men had been knocked down by arrows, the Welsh archers in a spirit of sanguinary democracy slipped out from behind the palisade to cut the throats of the immobilised French aristocracy. This was unpopular with the English aristocracy who not only felt a certain kinship, but also hoped to make some cash from ransoms.

The English and Welsh longbow was a weapon which, to be used effectively, demanded regular practice and considerable physical strength — a pull of over 100lbs (50kg) was required. War arrows recovered from the Mary Rose, which sank at Portsmouth in 1545, show a design which is close to that of a modern anti-tank (AT) round. The 3 foot (0.9 metre) shaft could be as thick as a .50" round, and was tipped with a sharp point — akin to a long rod penetrator in an AT round. This meant that enormous energy was focused into a small area, making it capable of penetrating armour.

Archers could adjust from dense long-range plunging fire — which fell among men and horses as they formed up and began their charge at 300 yards (274 metres) — to flat trajectory direct fire at 100 yards which would penetrate armour. A trained archer could fire ten rounds a minute, which meant that at Agincourt the 8,000 English and Welsh archers were putting 80,000 arrows a minute into the target area.

In 'A History of the English Speaking People', Winston Churchill records that the longbow was more accurate than most muskets up to the American Civil War in the 1860s. During World War II there was even serious discussion about the effectiveness of the bow as a silent weapon for killing enemy sentries. However to be an effective archer it was necessary for a man to practise almost daily and the musket, even though it was crude, slow and inaccurate, could be fired by a simple conscript soldier with a minimum of

The shoulder tab for the 2nd Ranger Battalion

training. New technology in the 15th Century included the Hussite War Wagons, which anticipated the function of armoured personnel carriers in the 20th Century, carrying infantry to battle in protected vehcles. Through the following centuries battles remained set piece actions, with infantry and field artillery holding the ground and cavalry providing the shock and manoeuvre element.

The Ranger tradition

Though European wars shaped military tactics and philosophy, a pointer to new tactics appeared in

North America between 1754 and 1763 in King George's War, also known as the French and Indian War. The Indian tribes with which the French and English had struck up alliances were excellent trackers, and used camouflage and sudden and violent ambush to defeat the medium-range firepower of muskets and the longer range of artillery.

The British were fortunate to have the services of Major Robert Rogers of Connecticut. Rogers' Rangers operated against the French and Indians and adopted many of the techniques used by the Indians. His most famous operation was against the Abenaki Indians whose capital was at St Francis, forty miles south of Montreal. With a force of 200 Rangers travelling by canoe and cross-country, Rogers covered 400 miles in 60 days. Though they had suffered losses during the journey, they reached St Francis without the enemy being aware of their presence. On 29 September 1759 they launched their attack, killing several hundred Indians and finishing the Abenaki as a force. Rogers was later commissioned into the 60th Foot (The Royal Americans). His 28 standing orders for the Rangers have been refined into 19 and with few exceptions are just as relevant today:

A Ranger radio operator on Grenada in 1983. His cap is shaped in the characteristic 'Ranger Crush'. He is armed with an M16 rifle.

Rogers' Rangers Standing Orders

1. Don't forget nothing.
2. Have your musket clean as a whistle, hatchet scoured, sixty rounds powder and ball, and be ready to march at a minute's warning.
3. When you're on the march act the way you would if you was sneaking up on a deer. See the enemy first.
4. Tell the truth about what you see and what you do. There is an army depending on us for correct information. You can lie all you please when you tell the folks about the Rangers, but don't never lie to a Ranger or an officer.
5. Don't never take a chance you don't have to.
6. When we're on the march we march single file, far enough apart so one shot can't go through two men.
7. If we strike swamps, or soft ground, we spread out abreast, so its hard to track us.
8. When we march, we keep moving till dark, so as to give the enemy the least possible chance at us.
9. When we camp, half the party stays awake while the other half sleeps.
10. If we take prisoners, we keep 'em separate till we have time to examine them, so they can't cook up a story between them.
11. Don't ever march home the same way. Take a

Rangers on patrol in a flooded area during a training exercise in the United States.

different route so you won't be ambushed.

12. No matter whether we travel in big parties or small ones, each party has to keep a scout about 20 yards on each flank, and 20 yards in the rear, so the main body can't be surprised and wiped out.

13. Every night you'll be told where to meet if surrounded by a superior force.

14. Don't sit down to eat without posting sentries.

15. Don't sleep beyond dawn. Dawn's when the French and Indians attack.

16. Don't cross a river by a regular ford.

17. If somebody's trailing you, make a circle, come back onto your own track, and ambush the folks that aim to ambush you.

18. Don't stand up when the enemy's coming against you. Kneel down, lie down, hide behind a tree.

19. Let the enemy come till he's almost close enough to touch. Then let him have it and jump out and finish him off with your hatchet.

The name Ranger dates back to reports by American Colonist soldiers who would say "This day ranged nine miles". Ranging meant travelling across some of the toughest terrain in the world. North America was a land of vast, thick forests, steep mountains and fast-flowing rivers, populated by hostile Indian tribes. The title Ranger has remained in the modern US Army.

Rangers fought for both sides during the Civil War

and later in the Mexican War. During World War II the title was revived and six Ranger battalions took part in raids in Europe and spearheaded landings there and in the Far East. The first WWII Ranger unit was formed at Carrickfergus, Northern Ireland, in 1942 under command of Major William Derby. The first US troops to fight on the European mainland were Rangers who landed with British Commandos at Dieppe in August 1942. Rangers fought in North Africa, Sicily and Italy including the landing at Salerno, and in the bloody battle for Cisterna the 1st and 3rd Ranger Battalions virtually ceased to exist.

At D-Day the Rangers won a motto and created a legend. At the Point du Hoc (actually Point du Hoe — it was incorrectly spelt on the US plans as Hoc, and the erroneous spelling has stuck) massive concrete positions had been identified, which it was feared held 155mm guns which could shell the US troops landing at Omaha and Utah beaches. Ranger Force A from the 2nd Battalion was tasked with a direct assault up cliffs to destroy the guns. When the force landed and stormed the cliffs they found the area heavily bomb damaged, but no guns. Only after they had penetrated inland did they discover four unmounted guns which they destroyed with thermite grenades.

For two days Ranger Force A held their own beach-head and fought off the German 914th Infantry Regiment, losing 135 dead and wounded out of a force of 225 men before they were relieved. Fifty years later veterans of the assault returned to the Point du Hoc and, to the awe of US Army Rangers young enough to be their grandchildren, climbed the cliff again.

At Dog White beach on Omaha, men of Ranger Force C, 2nd Ranger Battalion, were under cover of the sea wall when Brigadier General Norman Cota, assistant divisional commander of the 29th Infantry Division, demanded what unit they were. When he learned that they were Rangers, his yell "Rangers lead the way" galvanised them into action and sparked the US breakout from what had until then been a killing ground. "Rangers lead the way" has become the force motto.

In the Pacific the 6th Rangers took part in the landings on the Philippines and in a daring raid liberated over 500 American prisoners held at a PoW camp at Cabanatuan on Luzon. It was at D-Day on 6 June 1944 that the 2nd and 5th Rangers gave the title a new lustre and earned a Presidential Citation.

After World War II Ranger units were disbanded, but Ranger training continued as a qualification. The Ranger tab worn on the shoulder like a British Army

The bomb blasted casemates on the Point du Hoc in Normany which were the objective for the US Rangers in June 1944. They did not contain the 155mm guns which it was feared would bombard the D Day beaches.

regimental title became a highly prized qualification. Entry qualifications for the Rangers include passing a Medical and the Army Readiness Test. There is a three-week Airborne Course for those who are not jump qualified and then the three-week Ranger Indoctrination Programme or selection phase. This consists of infantry combat skills, reconnaissance and navigation, and ends with PT tests, timed runs and marches with full kit. Eight to twelve weeks follows

The red sand stone cliffs at the Point du Hoc which were scaled by Rangers on June 6, 1944. Allied bombers had cratered the edge of the cliff and reduced its height.

with a Ranger Company learning small unit tactics and basic combat skills. The Ranger Course over eight weeks covers physical tests, advanced patrolling skills, demolitions, fire support, reconnaissance, survival, and patrolling in different environments including the tropics and mountains. Students are introduced to airmobile and small boat operations. For soldiers who are airborne qualified the challenge is "Ranger training makes an Airborne soldier better".

Following the Vietnam War the US Army under

The Ranger memorial built on the roof of the battery observation post at the Point du Hoc.

The memorial at Omaha beach, Normany for the 5th Ranger Battalion, it was here that the Rangers won their slogan 'Rangers lead the way'.

General Creighton went through a tough period of reassessment. Morale was low and the experiment of the all-volunteer force was not attracting a notably high calibre of recruit. One of the changes instituted by Abrams was the formation of two light infantry Ranger battalions, the 1-75th and 2-75th. Many men who joined were already Ranger qualified, and the Ranger battalions set a standard through the US Army for training, physical fitness and discipline. The 1-75th and 2-75th saw action in Grenada in Operation Urgent Fury in 1983 and Operation Just Cause in Panama in 1989, when the two battalions parachuted in to seize the Rio Hato airfield 50 miles west of Panama City.

The Rifleman – a thinking soldier

Within European armies the concept of Light Infantry had caught on in the late 18th Century. These were men who worked as a screen of sharpshooters, forward of the main forces who would be drawn up in squares, lines or columns. The coincidence of technology and leadership produced a force which would dominate infantry actions during the Napoleonic wars. During this period British soldiers used the Brown Bess flintlock musket. This fired a .75" ball, but a soldier could not hit a man-sized target with it beyond 80 yards. The Baker Rifle

35

took longer to load and fired a .625" ball, but the rifling in the barrel ensured that it was accurate over longer ranges.

Leadership came from General Sir John Moore, who in 1800 raised The Experimental Corps of Riflemen (Later known as the Rifle Brigade they would, with the 43rd and 52nd Light Infantry, form the Light Brigade within the Light Division in Spain during the Peninsula War of 1808-14). The essence of Moore's training was to see soldiers not as pawns on the battlefield, to be shuttled about in blocks, but as intelligent men who could use initiative and small unit tactics. Scarlet uniforms and brass buttons were replaced with German-style dark hunting green tunics with black horn buttons. Men worked as skirmishing screens, using cover as camouflage and against fire. Bugles replaced drums for signalling in battle and no colours were carried since men would not fight in squares.

Interestingly when the men were required to stand and fight in the conventional style they were also highly effective. In Spain the Light Division, under attack by four Brigades of French cavalry, formed into five squares and withdrew over two miles sustaining only 35 casualties.

In Spain, Moore's ideal of common-sense and humanism was improved on by Major General

Robert 'Black Bob' Craufard. His Code of Standing
Orders, like the Standing Operational Procedures
(SOPs) of the 1990s, ensured that men reacted fast
and effectively. Captain John Kincaid noted: "The
value of all this became plain in the presence of the
enemy. Seven minutes sufficed to get the whole
division under arms in the middle of the night and
fifteen to bring it in order of battle to its alarm posts,
with the baggage loaded and assembled under escort
in the rear."

The Peninsula War was not only the proving ground
for new tactics and styles of training and leadership. It
marked the debut of the guerrilla — civilian soldiers
fighting an irregular war against an occupying force.
Over the centuries the guerrilla (from the Spanish
'little war'), partisan, resistance worker, freedom
fighter (or terrorist, depending on your point of view)
would fight with and against Special Forces. In Spain
the thinking soldiers of the Light Division working
with Spanish guerrillas gave Wellington's and Sir John
Moore's armies a screen which the French forces were
unable to penetrate.

Civil War cavalry raids

About fifty years after the Napoleonic Wars the
United States were torn apart by the Civil War of
1861-65. During that fifty years the Industrial

Revolution had changed Europe and the United States. The railroad allowed men and equipment to be moved in volume and at speeds undreamt of by Napoleon, Wellington or Suverov. The telegraph allowed the passage of information over vast distances. In sieges both sides dug trenches and there was even a modest use of barbed wire. Tethered balloons were used by Federal forces for air reconnaissance. The Union used its industrial might to mass-produce weapons, clothing, equipment and ships in volumes which could not be matched by the South. Though photographs had been taken during the Crimean War 1853-6, the role of the photographer as an accurate documenter of war came into its own during the Civil War.

These improvements, however, made large military forces — as well as the civilian infrastructure — much more vulnerable to attack by raiding parties or long range patrols. Telegraph lines and railroads could be cut, depots attacked and burned down, and road and rail bridges destroyed.

One of the most effective raiders of the Civil War was the Confederate James Ewell Brown 'Jeb' Stuart, who was only 28 years old when the Confederacy seceded. His first raid was during the Second Manassas (Bull Run). On 22 August 1862 he crossed the Rappahannock River with two guns and 1,500 troops. He attacked a Federal camp near Catlett's Station before sacking General Pope's baggage train. Under cover of a feint by the 1st and 5th Cavalry, Stuart escaped with 300 prisoners and valuable intelligence.

On two occasions in 1862 Stuart outflanked the lines of General McClellan and caused havoc in the Federal rear. Even when Stuart was in defence as part of the garrison of Fredericksburg, he led four sorties to capture supplies and ammunition.

Stuart was to die at the Battle of Yellow Tavern on 11 May 1864 when with 4,500 men he attempted to intercept a force of 10,000 Federal cavalry under Sheridan. Tragically he was killed by a shot from his own men — one of the earliest recorded examples of accidental fratricide or 'blue on blue'.

The exploits and style of Jeb Stuart have become part of the mythology of the Civil War. A less attractive character in the conflict is Jesse James, who during the war was a member of Quantrill's Raiders, a group of irregular Confederate cavalry. When the war ended he turned outlaw. His conduct and subsequent career highlights a feature of some men in Special Forces — when operations end and the licence to cause death and mayhem is withdrawn, some soldiers literally or psychologically self-destruct. In the words of a veteran of the Australian SAS quoting the film

Star Wars, they may "turn to the Dark Side of the Force" and use military skills for illegal or semi-criminal activities.

Commandos in action

The South African war of 1899-1902, between Afrikaans-speaking Boers and British and Imperial forces, had many of the features of the Civil War. Small arms and artillery had improved, rudimentary radios were transported by ox cart, and the heliograph was a fast and efficient means of signalling. Both British and Boer forces used cavalry and mounted infantry for patrolling and raids.

Boer militia forces were grouped into Commandos, a word taken from the Portuguese, and as the weight of numbers and improved British tactics forced the Boers onto the defensive, their Commandos adopted guerrilla tactics. The hardy Boers, who were excellent shots and good horsemen, sustained the war despite terrible hardships. The Boer civilian population who had provided support were put into concentration camps by the British, who used a system of block houses and barbed wire fences along railway tracks to restrict the movement of the Commandos. By May 1902 these tactics had worked and the Boers sued for peace.

The young Winston Churchill, working as a war

Armed with German 11mm Model 1871 Mauser rifles and early Winchesters a party of Boers observe Kimberley in 1899.

correspondent, had been captured by the Boers in 1899 and subsequently escaped. His admiration for his tough adversaries included a lasting friendship with a former Commando leader, soldier and statesman, General Jan Smuts. In June 1940, soon after the evacuation from Dunkirk, plans were drawn up in Britain to form groups of volunteers to conduct raids against German installations on the coast of Occupied Europe. Churchill was an enthusiastic advocate of the force and proposed they be called Commandos.

Lawrence of Arabia

The American Civil War is a pointer to the technology used in the wars of the 20th Century, and the slaughter of World War I demonstrated the inability of the professional military mind to grasp the killing power of science and technology.

The Great War, or 'War to end all wars', did however include original minds capable of employing tactics which used men and resources economically and tactics familiar to modern Special Forces.

One of these original minds belonged to Thomas Edward 'TE' Lawrence, who had worked in northern Syria before the war as an archaeologist, spoke Arabic, and had a keen understanding of the Arab tribal groupings and loyalties. Lawrence spent the first two years of the war working as an intelligence officer in Cairo. In 1916 he was sent to Jedda on a mission to Sherif Husain of Mecca and his son Feisal. The desire of the tribal groups to expel the Turks from the Arabian Peninsula and Palestine was to be harnessed by the British. Lawrence was directed to assist in the insurrection.

In many ways his operations are akin to those of Special Forces in the latter years of the 20th Century. He integrated with the tribal groups, wearing Arab clothes and riding camels, but he also brought British

Camels with the Transport Corps on the Palestinian Front are watered by their Arab handlers. TE Lawrence was an experienced camel rider which stood him in good stead with his Arab comrades.

equipment and expertise. British Army Stokes mortar and Lewis light machine gun instructors trained the Arabs, and Lawrence used high explosives to attack track and rolling stock in ambushes on the Hejaz Railway. This railway was an important strategic link running from Turkey, via Damascus in Syria, Amman in trans Jordan, to Medina in what is now Saudi

43

Arabia. The Turks had garrisoned it at stations and water points, and sent armed trains to protect the track. Attacks, using explosives, small arms and light machine gun fire, not only produced arms and booty, but also depressed Turkish morale and raised that of the Arabs.

Jungle fighters

In Africa a German, Colonel Paul von Lettow-Vorbeck, led Imperial German forces in East Africa. From the outbreak of World War I he never had more than 3,000 Germans and 11,000 native Askaris, but held at bay a force of British and Imperial troops numbering 130,000. In November 1917 the main body of his forces were captured, but von Lettow-Vorbeck led his survivors in Portuguese East Africa (Angola), where he captured rations and ammunition off the startled garrison of Portuguese, whose country had declared for the Allies in 1916.

Von Lettow Vorbeck was able to live off the land until 1918 when he moved northwards into Northern Rhodesia (Zambia), surrendering on 23 November — twelve days after the end of the war. Though his force was too small to protect the German colonies in Africa, he used it to tie up British and Imperial forces which would have otherwise been deployed in the Middle East or Western Front.

Improvising hand grenades from ration tins during a quiet moment behind the lines in World War I. Raids and special operations during World War I were not as sophisticated as operations in World War II.

Stormtroopers

On the Western Front between 1915 and 1916 the Germans developed groups called Storm Troops which were squads of trained trench fighters from within infantry regiments. The Sturm-Bataillone comprised two to four companies with machine gun, flame-thrower and Minenwerfer (heavy mortar) companies. They were used for assaults and counter-attacks. The battalions were dispersed later in the war since they creamed off the best men from infantry

45

units, the quality of which consequently suffered. This fear — that taking volunteers for elite units would dilute the quality of conventional forces — has always coloured attitudes to Special Forces.

The pitted concrete at the entrance to the Belgian fort of Eben Emael neutralised by a German airborne attack in 1940.

Downstream from Eben Emael German Army pioneers cross the bridge at Canne over the Albert canal. It was the only bridge successfully destroyed, others were captured by glider borne troops.

Hitler's Special Forces

Nazi Germany, Fascist Italy and Communist Russia were pioneers with airborne forces between the wars. The image of paratroops, futuristic soldiers descending from the sky, fitted with that of new revolutionary political systems which were galvanising the world. n 1940 German daring paid off at the

47

A German Army flame thrower crew in action at Eben Emael. Though the glider borne troops had neutralised the fort, it had not surrendered and did so after pioneers attacked from outside.

Belgian fortress of Eben Emael which guarded vital bridges at the confluence of the deep Albert canal and Maas river not far from Liege. Following the lessons of World War I, where fighting a defensive battle from fortifications had produced fewer casualties, the French had built the Maginot Line and the Belgians dug the Albert Canal as a huge anti-tank ditch, with

As German infantry take a break the defeated Belgian garrison awaits it fate at Eben Emael.

the ultra-modern Eben Emael covering its approaches. The fort had over a kilometre of tunnels, with its own power and water supply and nine 7.5cm guns in turrets. For the men of Army Group B pushing into Belgium in May 1940, Eben Emael was a major

49

obstacle. The Germans neutralised the fort by landing 85 men in eleven DFS 230 gliders within its perimeter on 10 May. The men were Luftwaffe combat engineer troops from the 1st Parachute Regiment. Their demolition equipment included previously unknown devices called shaped charges, which contained 50kg of explosives and were capable of penetrating concrete and armour. Working from turret to turret they neutralised guns and demoralised the garrison.

A day later ground troops crossed the Albert canal and linked up, and the fort surrendered. The German troops, commanded by Lieutenant Witzig, suffered six killed and 15 wounded, the Belgians 23 dead and 59 wounded.

Coup de main operations were an essential part of the German success during the early years of the war. Rejecting the static defensive strategy of the French, Dutch and Belgians, they adopted fast mechanised tactics, with tanks and armoured personnel carriers (APCs) supported by dive bombers. To ensure that the enemy did not demolish bridges and so delay the advance, Brandenburgers, Army special forces tasked

Graves and battered embrasures at Eben Emael, the photographs from the German magazine Signal do not show the effect of hollow charges on the armoured turrets, which demoralised the Belgian gunners.

Après
l'assaut

A still from film of German pioneers crossing the Albert canal under fire from Eben Emael.

by the Abwehr, penetrated ahead of the attacks, often disguised in enemy uniforms. Brandenburgers saw action in Belgium and Holland and the invasion of the USSR in 1941. One man, dirty and utterly exhausted and still in his Red Army uniform, was filmed by a Propagandakompanie as an example of "Soviet sub-humans". Brandenburgers also conducted long range patrols in North Africa.

As the war moved against them, the Germans found

that allies like Italy and Hungary were keen to escape from their alliances and side with the United States and United Kingdom. When in July 1943 Italy changed sides and arrested its former leader, the Duce Benito Mussolini, the German leader Adolf Hitler was adamant that his friend should be located and released.

SS Commandos

German radio interception traced Mussolini to a mountain-top hotel at Gran Sasso. The hotel could only be reached by a mountain railway, so a direct assault was impossible. However with Mussolini's location established Otto Skorzeny, a colourful character and a Lieutenant Colonel in the Waffen-SS, was tasked with his rescue. In great secrecy on 12 September, Skorzeny took 12 DFS 230 gliders with 20 Luftwaffe paratroops and 50 Waffen-SS commandos. Four aircraft dropped out, but the remaining force made a dramatic landing on the small plateau close to the hotel. Paratroopers and Waffen-SS men charged into the hotel, destroyed its radio links and in less than four minutes and for no loss on either side had located and liberated Mussolini. Skorzeny and the Duce then made a hazardous exit from Gran Sasso by Fieseler Storch reconnaissance aircraft.

In October 1944 Skorzeny led the team which

SS-Sturmbannfuhrer Otto Skorzeny sporting his Knights Cross, his duelling scar earned him the nickname 'Scarface Skorzeny' with American forces.

kidnapped the son of Admiral Horthy, the Regent and national leader of Hungary, who was forced to resign. This ensured that Hungary did not defect to the USSR and continued to supply oil for the dwindling German armoured and mechanised forces.

Germans wearing US uniform

At the close of the year Skorzeny led a group of Special Forces designated Panzer Brigade 150. The force consisted of 390 men dressed in US Army uniforms and travelling in Jeeps. Skorzeny had called for volunteers with good idiomatic American English and knowledge of military slang. He got the men he wanted — just ten of them. Of the remainder, 30 had a good knowledge of English, 150 could understand it, and 200 had a command of a few phrases.

Their mission was to precede the German ground attack in the Ardennes in Belgium in December 1944, infiltrate US Army lines and gather intelligence and cause confusion by changing road signs, issuing false orders to convoys, and removing minefield markers. The men, in seven teams, wore German uniforms beneath their GI disguises. They were told by a German lawyer that this was an acceptable ruse

55

L Cpl Manfred Pernass one of Skorzeny's disguised commandos captured by the Americans during the Ardennes offensive in 1944-45 moments before his execution with two other comrades.

A special issue of Signal celebrates the rescue of Benito Mussolini from the ski hotel at Gran Sasso by paratroopers and Waffen-SS men under command of Otto Skorzeny in September 1943.

Signal

Un communiqué historique: effect les mainstr ordonne a la garde de l'hôtel Otto Skorzeny, qui conduisit l'entreprise de libération du Duce. Désorientés et efficaces les carabinieri obéirent aussitôt.

La libération de Mussolini

Mussolini in hat and overcoat makes his way to the little Fieseler Fi 156 Storch observation aircraft which flew him off the plateau at Gran Sasso.

of war, as long as they did not engage in combat in enemy uniforms. The US Army thought otherwise — they saw the men as spies and executed those who were captured.

Interestingly these tactics would have been used against NATO in a ground war by the Special Forces of the National Volks Armee (NVA), the East German Army. They would have been dressed and equipped as men of the West German Bundeswehr and would have travelled in US M113 APCs which

German rescuers and Italian former gaolers wave off Skorzeny and Mussolini on a rather hazardous flight.

had been captured in Vietnam and which had been repainted as Bundeswehr vehicles.

Skorzeny's commandos caused enormous confusion with GIs attempting to establish the true identity of even senior officers at checkpoints by asking detailed questions about sports and film stars and other arcane information known only to a native American. At one checkpoint even General Omar Bradley was required to list the former husbands of a much-married Hollywood star. The German commandos had some operational successes, bluffing infantry into withdrawing and blowing up an ammunition dump.

Unintentionally the German Jeep patrols added to the confusion, for many of their men believed that the

59

real mission of Panzer Brigade 150 was to kill General Dwight Eisenhower, the commander in chief of the Anglo-American forces in Europe. When they were captured and blurted out this rumour, Eisenhower in the safety of Paris was put under a close guard.

Werewolf: Nazi Resistance in 1945

The final attempt by Nazi Germany to use Special Forces was the rather theatrically named Werewolf. As the Allies captured German territory it was hoped that German resistance groups would attack convoys and assassinate collaborators. Training centres were set up in Germany and Austria. Werewolves were largely very young fanatical Nazis; older people had become war weary. They had some success, killing the commander of the 3rd Armoured Division, Major General Maurice Rose, on 24 March 1945, and the Allied appointed Mayor of Aachen.

The death of General Rose hardened attitudes and any attempts at ambushes were met with heavy fire. On 5 June two Hitler Youth aged 16 and 17 accused of sniping were executed by firing squad. With the end of the war in 1945, Werewolf died.

British Commandos

Immediately after the evacuation at Dunkirk in 1940, the British Prime Minister, Winston Churchill,

10th Commandos in training practice cliff assault techniques. The ability to ascend cliffs allowed landings to be made in on beaches which did not look obvious to the Germans.

proposed that Commandos take the war back to German occupied Europe. Men were drawn from the Royal Marines and the Army: the former had the advantage of experience with amphibious operations, but the Army were quick learners.

At the same time that Commandos were being raised, Airborne forces were being selected and trained. There was a drive to break down the barriers between the Royal Navy (RN), Army and Royal Air Force (RAF) to conduct Combined Operations. To reinforce this co-operation a red and dark blue flash was designed which featured the anchor for the RN, Thompson sub-machine gun for the Army, and an eagle for the RAF. This badge was worn during the War and after 1945 by Royal Marines and the RN and RAF teams working with them. With an SA80 rifle replacing the Thompson, it became the campaign medal for British land, sea and air force personnel who fought in the Gulf War of 1990-91.

Probably the finest example of Combined Ops (Operations) was Operation Biting which took place on the night of 27 February 1942. RAF aerial photographs of the French coast showed a German Wurzburg early warning and fire control radar in a remote location at Bruneval near Le Havre. A company strength force, under command of Major John Frost, was drawn from the 2nd Battalion the Parachute Regiment and 1st Parachute Squadron Royal Engineers, with Flight Lieutenant Cox, an RAF radar technician. That night they parachuted into France from 12 modified Whitley bombers, a few miles inland from Bruneval. They quickly made their

The definitive image of the war time Commando with his Fairburn Sykes knife. The FS knife remains one of the classic fighting knife designs.

way to the site and, as different parties neutralised the crew and garrison, the Royal Engineers and the RAF expert dismantled components from the radar.

At 0215hrs they moved down a gully to the beach and waited for RN small vessels to evacuate them. There was a nerve racking delay as the RN vessels avoided a German destroyer and then they made their run in. By dawn the men and their radar booty were safely back in Portsmouth harbour. The operation had cost two killed, six wounded who were evacuated, and six missing, but it had netted invaluable technical equipment.

At that time the British Government Communications HQ (GCHQ) was located at Swanage on the Dorset coast. Understandably in 1942 there was a fear that the Germans might conduct a similar type of operation against Swanage, so GCHQ was moved to the security of inland Cheltenham, where it remained after the war.

British Commando raids against Europe and North Africa were constrained by the number of suitable targets which were close to the coast but not too heavily defended. Successes were chalked up with attacks on 4 March and 27 December 1941 against the Lofoten Islands in Norway. The targets included fish oil factories and the opportunity to take prisoners. The island of Vaagso, 100 miles north of

Lt Dennis O'Flaherty wounded in the Vaagso Commando raid in December 1941. One of the men supporting him is armed with a Boys anti-tank rifle.

Bergen, was raided on 12 December 1941 and though Commando casualties were severe the principal targets were destroyed. On a strategic scale the Commando operations convinced Hitler that Norway was a potential target for a large-scale invasion. He ordered resources be directed to building coastal defences and by 1944 the garrison stood at over 350,000 troops.

Some Commando raids involved just a few men —

65

A captured French 75mm field gun part of a four gun battery used by the Germans for local defence on Maaloy island , off Vaagso is examined by men of 6 Troop prior to its destruction.

like that by the Small Scale Raiding Force at 0125hrs on 2 September 1942 against the Casquets lighthouse, six miles west of the Channel Island of Alderney. The force was rather over-officered, consisting of ten officers — including the Dane Anders Lassen VC, MC and two bars — and two men. They surprised two Germans who were supposedly on watch and five others in bed. Prisoners,

A Royal Navy landing craft is readied to receive casualties and Commandos following the Vaagso raid.

code books and diaries were captured and radio equipment destroyed, for no losses.

The St. Nazaire raid

Earlier in 1942 the scale of operations changed dramatically with Operation Charioteer, an attack on the French port of St Nazaire which had become a German naval and U-boat base. The aim of the attack was to destroy the dry dock lock gates and port facilities so they could not be used by the German warship Tirpitz, then in Norway.

The raid, on the morning of 28 March, was conducted by 268 volunteers from No 2 Commando, commanded by the pipe smoking Lt Col Charles Newman. The 18 small coastal assault craft and the ex-US destroyer HMS Cambeltown were commanded by Commander Robert Ryder RN. The destroyer was packed with three tons of explosives, and rammed into the gates of the dry docks. Commandos raced ashore to destroy the winding gear for the gates and attempted to neutralise the U-boat pens.

It was a violent and costly night in which only two assault craft escaped; 169 Commandos were killed and 200 taken prisoner. Both Ryder and Newman were taken prisoner and learned later in Prisoner of War (PoW) camp that they had been awarded Britain's highest award for gallantry, the Victoria Cross (VC). The VC also went to Able Seaman Savage who had manned his 20mm Oerlikon gun throughout the operation, silencing German guns, until he was mortally wounded.

In the morning, as senior German officers were inspecting the wreck of HMS Cambeltown, the three tons of amatol in the bow detonated. The lock gates were shattered and the remains of the destroyer was carried half-way down the dock. Tirpitz never left Norway.

Survivors return from the Dieppe raid, a disaster which led to the decision to make the D-Day landings across open beaches, not heavily-defended ports.

Disaster at Dieppe

The attack on Dieppe in August 1942 was codenamed Op Jubilee. Before the operation Admiral Lord Louis Mountbatten, head of Combined Operations, said this was not a raid but "an act of war". It involved 5,000 men from the 2nd Canadian Division, with 1,000 men from Nos 3 and 4 Commando. The landings were to take place on eight

69

Amphibous landing craft were tested in action by a series of commando raids on the German-held coasts of Europe.

beaches, supported by 28 Churchill tanks of the Calgary Regiment. The aim was to destroy batteries and other installations before withdrawal.

Despite awesome bravery, the Canadians' assault on the shingle beaches in front of Dieppe was stopped almost before they left their landing craft. They lost 3,164 men and 215 officers as well as all their tanks. The Royal Navy lost 81 officers and 4,699 men killed, as well as the destroyer HMS Berkley.

The only success was on the flanks where No 4

Commandos return from a raid. They were so successful that Hitler ordered any captured members of British Special Forces to be murdered by the Gestapo.

Commando silenced the Hess battery, while No 3 Commando kept up steady sniper fire on the Goebbels battery which prevented it firing on the warships and landing craft off Dieppe. No 4 Commando included some of the 44 US Rangers who had completed their training in Achnacarry in Scotland. One of their number, Corporal Koons, became the first US soldier to kill an enemy in Europe. He was awarded the Silver

71

Following the Dieppe raid in August 1942 Commandos clean their .303 SMLE rifles. They may be men of No 4 Commando who attacked the Hess battery to the west of Dieppe.

Star and received the Military Medal from the British. When the US newspapers learned that Rangers had landed at Dieppe one of them splashed a huge headline "Yanks invade Europe". The Commandos lost 24 officers and 223 men during the Dieppe operation.

With some justification the Germans claimed Dieppe as a victory; for British planners it was described as a "reconnaissance in force" from which valuable lessons were learned and applied at D-Day on 6 June 1944. Specialised armoured vehicles were developed for breaching sea walls, neutralising strongpoints and crossing gaps.

Long Range Desert Group

In North Africa the Long Range Desert Group (LRDG) and No 1 Demolition Squadron, better known as Popski's Private Army (PPA), took the war to the Axis alongside the SAS. PPA was given its name by Lt Col Shan Hackett who was at that time co-ordinator of Special Forces. Popski was Vladimir Peniakoff, a white Russian who had lived and worked in the Middle East before the war. His 'private army' never exceeded 80 men and, like the SAS, he used Jeeps as his transport. When the war in North Africa was over it looked as if PPA would be disbanded, but Peniakoff enjoyed excellent contacts and the force survived to operate behind enemy lines in Italy up to 1945.

The Long Range Desert Group could trace its origins back to British operations in World War I. Desert driving and navigation skills were kept alive

with military expeditions led by Major Ralph
Bagnold. In June 1940 when the Italians declared war
on Britain, Bagnold proposed that his experienced
crews conduct operations into Italian controlled
Libya. The LRDG was essentially an intelligence
gathering force, but teamed up with the SAS to
provide transportation to and from targets. In 1945
the highly experienced group was disbanded.

Airborne and Special Forces played an important
part in the D-Day landings, including the capture of
the bridges over the river Orne and the Caen canal by
glider-borne men of the Oxfordshire and
Buckinghamshire Light Infantry. Paratroopers
attacked coastal gun positions as well as securing the
flanks of the invasion beaches.

The Chindits

The defeats suffered by the US Army in the
Philippines, and by the British and Commonwealth
in Malaya and Singapore in 1941-42, gave the
Japanese sea, land and air forces a reputation for
invincibility. Japanese forces had pushed through
Malaya and Burma and were on the borders of India.

Success against the Japanese came in 1943 when
men from the 77th Indian Infantry Brigade, under
command of Major General Orde Wingate, launched
an overland deep-penetration raid into Burma. The

The C-47 Dakota which delivered paratroopers and special forces to DZs in Europe and the Far East. It was a vital link in the Second Chindit operation.

Brigade consisted of the 13th King's Liverpool Regiment, 3/2nd Gurkha Rifles, 142 Commando and long range signals.

Wingate had already led Ethiopian insurgents in a group called Gideon Force against the Italians in the 1940-41 campaign in Abyssinia, and was a forceful advocate of operations conducted deep in the enemy's rear.

Wingate's force were called Chindits after their

75

sleeve flash showing a chinthe — a stone lion which guarded the entrance to Burmese temples. To penetrate Japanese held Burma the Chindits were divided into Company strength columns with pack mules. Re-supply was by parachute drop. Initially what became the First Chindit Expedition enjoyed success, destroying a railway line and blasting a gorge to block the track with rocks and rubble. The Japanese and the harsh climate took a heavy toll on the force, however, and by the time it had returned overland to India it had shrunk from 3,000 to 2,182, of whom only 600 were adjudged fit for frontline service. It was a high cost, but British and Commonwealth forces were no longer on the defensive.

Wingate enjoyed considerable celebrity and the Second Chindit Expedition received considerably more resources. It was expanded into six brigades from the 3rd Indian Division and assisted by the United States Army Air Force. It was split into 300-strong columns and delivered by Waco glider to landing zones (LZs) deep in the jungle. Here defensive positions were constructed and airstrips

Brigadier Charles Orde Wingate: the inspiration for the two Chindit operations which penetrated behind Japanese lines in Burma in 1943 and 1944.

built to evacuate casualties.

The expedition was timed to disrupt the Japanese U-GO offensive against Imphal and Kohima. It cut supply lines and tied up the equivalent of two-and-a-half Japanese divisions. The Chindits were then directed north to assist Lt Gen Joseph 'Vinegar Joe' Stilwell's Chinese American army, the advance of which had been stalled by the stubborn Japanese defence of Myitkyina.

Following Wingate's death in an air crash on 24 March 1944, command passed to General Walter Lentaigne. Lentaigne conducted the rest of the campaign with skill and determination, even though he attracted criticism from General Stilwell who did not understand that the Chindits were now exhausted and suffering from ill health.

Criticism that the formation of the Chindits, like Special Forces in Europe, drew off the cream of soldiers in the British 14th Army is unfounded. What made the performance of the two expeditions remarkable was that the regiments employed were not elite formations, but were well trained and led line infantry.

A charismatic if eccentric leader, Wingate with beard and topee takes his ease on a Dakota which has been fitted out to carry mules.

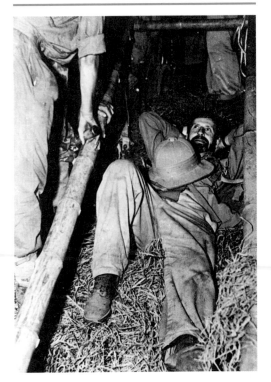

Merrill's Marauders

In northern Burma the US Army deployed a force with the rather cumbersome title of 5307th Composite Unit (Provisional), under the command of Brigadier General Frank Merrill. They were dubbed 'Merrill's Marauders' by Time/Life war correspondent James Shepley. Merrill had served as Military Attache in Tokyo before the war. He spoke Japanese and seemed well qualified for this testing command. The soldiers who made up the 2,000 Marauders were volunteers from the US Army Pacific and Caribbean Commands. Many were fine men, but within the group were some who merely wanted to get back to the United States, and some who suffered from psychiatric disorders.

Once they were committed to action they suffered from many of problems that beset the Chindits. Fatigue, disease and poor diet took their toll, and Merrill himself suffered two heart attacks and was temporarily evacuated. The Marauders fought in the Hukawng Valley in northern Burma, but when they were ordered by Stilwell to take the airfield and transportation centre of Myitkyina in May 1944, the enemy strength was too great. The town eventually fell, but by then the Marauders were so under-strength that they were withdrawn from the line.

Soviet Partisans

The Red Army employed scouts, snipers and reconnaissance troops at local levels, but small specialised groups did not fit into the collective ideals of Communism.

The ground operations of the Soviet Army were supported by Partisan attacks in the German rear areas, and these were backed up by air drops and infiltrated agents. In many ways the partisans were sufficiently effective that there was no need for Special Forces. Under guidance from Moscow they launched the War of the Railways in which they attacked the German transportation network. At the height of the operations in 1942 the Partisans numbered 150,000 to 200,000 men and women, and the Germans had deployed 25 Special Security divisions, as well as 30 infantry regiments and 100 battalions of police to combat them.

Winning the 'Hearts and Minds' of the local population was to play an important part in SAS operations after the war, but it had no place on the Eastern Front. Prisoners were a liability for Partisans, and German and Axis units executed prisoners with the grim mathematics that ten Russians were worth the life of one German soldier.

Kamikaze

Japanese special forces included their parachute arm, which was used during the invasion of the Dutch East Indies in 1942. At the close of the war Japanese soldiers, sailors and airmen — who had been imbued with the idea that surrender was dishonourable — were exhorted to die for their Emperor. The most dramatic manifestation of this was the men of the Special Attack Corps, better known as Kamikaze pilots (Kamikaze means Divine Wind, after a storm which destroyed a 13th Century Mongol invasion) The pilots flew their bomb-laden aircraft into US Navy, and later Royal Navy, warships in the Pacific. Six major Allied warships were sunk by Kamikaze attacks. Imperial Japanese Navy exponents of the ideal included torpedoes which were piloted by humans. On land the humble soldier became a human anti-tank mine, waiting in a hole in the road with an artillery shell which he detonated as the tank passed over him.

The Kamikaze approach to war was unique, but does not fit the style of operation by Western Special Forces. Some missions may be very hazardous, with men knowing that their chances may be slim, but they do not embark on them with the intention of killing themselves along with their enemy.

Japan's kamikaze suicide pilots sank 21 US warships off Okinawa in an estimated 3,000 one-way missions. Here, a US Navy carrier burns after a direct hit.

Special Air Service

Chapter 2: Special Air Service

The original concept of the Special Air Service —
small raiding forces capable of simultaneous attacks
on vulnerable airfields and logistics bases behind
enemy lines — was the brainchild of David Stirling, a
24-year-old Scots Guards subaltern. However credit
must also go to General Claude Auchinleck, then
Commander in Chief in North Africa, and his
Deputy Chief of Staff, Gen Neil Ritchie. In 1941
Stirling had bluffed his way into Ritchie's office to
present his idea for raiding forces. To the credit of
both generals they did not order the young officer
out, but saw the potential of his idea. Stirling felt that
the battalion-sized Commandos that were being
formed early in the war for amphibious raiding were
too cumbersome for covert operations, and that small
patrols would be able to penetrate enemy bases by
stealth, and attack using delayed action charges.

He was given permission to raise 60 men for what
would be called L Detachment Special Air Service
(SAS) Brigade. The title SAS Brigade was chosen in
order to convince German intelligence that the 8th
Army had an airborne brigade in theatre. As Chapter
1 shows, the formation of the SAS in North Africa
reflected a British and Commonwealth penchant for
'private armies' which produced Commandos, the
LRDG, Chindits and Popski's Private Army. For
Auchinleck the selection of 60 volunteers for the SAS

Lt Colonel David Stirling with a Jeep mounted SAS patrol. The vehicles have twin Vickers K machine guns as well as spare fuel and water. Personal kit is stowed at the rear.

would not deplete the strength and resources of the 8th Army, but their use behind enemy lines might cause confusion during a major offensive.

The force that was raised was later nicknamed the 'Originals' and included Lieutenant (Lt) John 'Jock' Lewes, who was an explosives expert, and Lt 'Paddy' Blair Mayne, an Irish rugby international with an explosive temper, but a superb soldier. Many of the

87

men in L Detachment were Commando trained ex-Guardsmen. This connection between the Brigade of Guards and the SAS remained after the War with the formation G Squadron 22 SAS which has a large number of Guardsmen.

Training and selection for the SAS was tough, and included a rudimentary parachute course. Two men died when their parachutes malfunctioned; after the problem had been resolved, Stirling was first out of the aircraft on the next training jump. Weapon training with Axis small arms, and desert survival and navigation, brought the force to a high standard.

Who Dares Wins

Despite accidents, the force enjoyed high morale and produced its own cap badge and parachute 'wings'. The motto 'Who Dares Wins' is reported to have been chosen by Stirling himself. The winged dagger, produced by Sergeant Bob Tait, was the winning design in a competition. One version of its origin is that the dagger was meant to be King Arthur's sword, Excalibur, but when the Egyptian tailor had embroidered it, the weapon looked like a dagger. Since Commandos and other special forces were using the Sykes Fairburn (SF) dagger, a winged dagger it became.

The distinctive dark blue and light blue SAS

SAS wings which incorporate the colours of Oxford and Cambridge and were based on ancient Egyptian designs.

parachute wings were designed by Jock Lewes who rowed for Oxford. He incorporated light blue since another Original, Lt Langton, had rowed for Cambridge. The shape of the wings is based on the ancient Egyptian paintings of scarabs. The original beret was white, but this was derided by the Australians and New Zealanders in the force and replaced by a khaki forage cap. The beige beret was introduced later in the war.

The first operation by L Detachment took place on the night of 16-17 November 1941, and was intended as one of the diversions during Operation Crusader. Sixty-five men were parachuted from five Bristol Bombay bombers. They were to split into patrols and make their way on foot to attack Axis aircraft using the Lewes bomb, a blast incendiary devised by Jock Lewes.

After the attack the men were to withdraw to a rendezvous (RV) with LRDG vehicles for extraction to Allied lines. However, on the night high winds scattered the aircraft, no attacks were made, many men were injured and only 22 men returned. Among those of the originals who were captured was Lt Charles Bonnington. Bad weather forced his aircraft to make an emergency landing, it took off again and en route to Tobruk was hit by flak and pursued by an enemy fighter. The Bristol Bombay crashed, killing the crew and one SAS man. After a grim four years as a PoW, including a time in manacles, Bonnington returned to the UK. After the war his son, Sir Christian Bonnington, became a highly respected Himalayan climber.

Stirling realised that parachuting was an unreliable mode of insertion and teamed up with the LRDG who had set up a base at Jalo (or Gialo) about 240km south of Benghazi, west of the Great Sand Sea in Cyrenaica. Operating from Jalo, Stirling and Mayne would lead nine men in an attack on the airfield at

A US Army Jeep straight from the factory, in use with the SAS it was extensively modified to save weight and increase stowage capacity.

Sirte, while Lewes would go for El Agheila on 14 December 1941 and Lt Bill Fraser would attack Agedabia a week later. On a night-time close reconnaissance of his target, Stirling disturbed the Italian occupants of the airfield, who evacuated it the following day. Mayne had better luck, placing bombs in 20 aircraft in 15 minutes. As an afterthought, Mayne kicked open the door of the officers' mess and fired a magazine of 30 rounds from his .45 Thompson sub-machine gun at the startled occupants. During the withdrawal Mayne spotted an aircraft that had not been attacked and, climbing into the cockpit, he ripped out a section of the instruments with his bare hands. It was an episode which would become part of SAS folklore. Mayne returned to the airfield twelve days later with a party of five men and destroyed a further 27 enemy aircraft.

Lewes found that his airfield was only a staging post and had no aircraft, so he used his 30 bombs on parked trucks. Fraser's attack was even more successful, destroying 37 Italian CR42 fighter bombers.

Over 100 aircraft destroyed

By the end of 1941 the SAS had destroyed more than 100 enemy aircraft, but tragically Jock Lewes had been killed in an air attack on his convoy. Lt Fraser and his patrol were reported missing but, after a 350km march lasting two weeks, they returned to Allied lines.

Stirling and Mayne were promoted to Major and Captain respectively, awarded DSOs by Auchinleck, and authorised to expand their force by a further 40 men. Among those who joined were a group of expert swimmers and canoeists from the reconnaissance section of Layforce. The Special Boat Section (SBS) allowed the SAS to launch operations against ports,

A post-war Belgian SAS vehicle: the Vickers K guns have been replaced with belt-fed 7.62mm MAG machine guns, with a MAG in a rear gunner's position which can be dismounted and used in the ground role. Armoured glass windscreens give protection .

and were later to be a significant force in the Aegean. They started operations in June 1942 when a party of the SBS under command of Earl George Jellicoe were taken by submarine to the north coast of Crete and paddled to the coast in rubber boats. They landed and destroyed 21 enemy aircraft at Heraklion.

Commandant (Maj) George Berge of the Free French, with 50 French paratroopers, also joined the SAS, where they were formed into a separate squadron. The French, along with Special Interrogation Group personnel disguised as Germans and driving captured enemy vehicles, attempted to penetrate the defences of Martuba airfield on 13 June 1942. The ruse was betrayed by an ex-Afrika Korps soldier in the group, and all but two of the party were captured. French SAS troops were later to play an important part in operations in France prior to and immediately after D-Day.

Using 15 Jeeps, with 3-ton trucks for logistic back up, the SAS launched their first raid against Bagysh airfield on 7 July 1942. The Axis forces were now alerted to the covert attacks with Lewes bombs, and had placed sentries around the aircraft. The SAS had also had the frustrating experience of some bombs failing to detonate after they had been placed in aircraft.

Stirling and Mayne therefore opted for a cavalry charge attack using the firepower of the armed Jeeps. That night three Jeeps careered down the runway firing at the parked aircraft. They returned safely and left behind them 37 burning aircraft.

Having proved the tactic, Stirling decided to attack the airfield at Sidi Haneish using a V shaped formation of two columns of seven Jeeps commanded respectively by Earl George Jellicoe and Paddy Mayne. They were to drive down the runway engaging the lines of aircraft parked on each side. On the night of 26 July 1942 they arrived at the airfield to find that the landing lights were on. They hit the airfield at speed and in minutes destroyed 40 Ju-52 transports. They lost two men killed, one wounded and two Jeeps destroyed.

1 SAS Regiment

By the close of the year, L Detachment was given full regimental status as 1 SAS Rgt. Further volunteers came from 8 Commando, and 121 men of the Greek special operations force Sacred Squadron. Stirling favoured the inclusion of Greeks within the force, since he saw a role for the SAS in the Greece and the Aegean. The Greeks were later attached to the SBS and fought in the Aegean. 1 SAS, with a strength of 601 men, was now organised into four squadrons: A, B, C (the Free French) and D (the SBS).

The huge open spaces of the desert gave the SAS an area into which they could withdraw after operations. In 1943, as the Axis forces were compressed into Tunisia, this space was reduced and SAS operations began to suffer. In January 1943 Colonel Stirling, now a Lieutenant, was captured in Tunisia. He had been attempting to lead a small group through Tunisia to meet up with the British 1st Army attacking east from Algeria. He was initially sent to the Italian Prisoner-of-War (PoW) camp at Gavi, but after four escape attempts he was shipped to the maximum security PoW camp at Colditz.

During operations in North Africa the SAS, under command of David Stirling, had destroyed over 400 enemy aircraft and tied up large numbers of troops protecting air bases and lines of communication. In 1990 Stirling was knighted but he died later that year.

When David Stirling was captured, command of the SAS passed to his brother, Lt Col William Stirling. William had raised 2 SAS and, though more systematic than his brother, he correctly perceived the raiding role of the SAS. It was pressure from the planners of Operation Overlord, the invasion of northern Europe, that later led William to resign: the planners perceived the SAS as akin to the Commandos and planned to use them with operations close behind the D-Day beach-head. If they had been employed in this role they would have been destroyed in days by the heavily armed and armoured German garrisons.

Special Raiding Squadron

D-Day was a year away, and the Allies would have a hard fight for Sicily and Italy. Though 2 SAS survived

Italian Partisans at the close of the War. SAS patrols worked with them in northern Italy harassing the withdrawing German forces.

in Algeria as a recruit training and selection organisation, 1 SAS was disbanded. Paddy Mayne's A Squadron was combined with the remnants of B and became the 250-strong Special Raiding Squadron

(SRS). D Squadron retained the SBS title and, as an independent unit using Greek fishing boats and small craft, conducted operations throughout the Mediterranean and Aegean. The French and Greek personnel were returned to their national armies.

The SRS were used in a direct assault Commando-style operation during the landings in Sicily in July 1943. They neutralised two Italian coastal artillery positions at Capo Murro di Porco. They were then withdrawn and in a second amphibious operation captured Augusta harbour.

The first operation of the SRS on the European mainland was on 3 September 1943 against the port of Bagnara in Southern Italy. Codenamed Baytown, the operation went badly when one of the Royal Navy landing craft broke down and the other ran ashore. Men and equipment had to be transferred to four much smaller craft which then landed on the wrong side of the bay. Initially there was only light resistance, but the Germans reacted quickly with machine gun and mortar fire. The SRS fought a series of actions for three days before Allied forces advancing from Reggio made contact with them. The SRS suffered five killed and 17 wounded.

On 3 October Operation Devon took 207 men of the SRS with two Commandos of the Special Service Brigade to Termoli. They cleared the town and had contacted the advancing reconnaissance patrols of the Lancashire Fusiliers and 2 SAS, when on the morning of the 5th the Germans put in a massive counter attack. After heavy fighting the day was saved by the arrival of Canadian Sherman tanks and men of the Royal Irish Rangers. After this operation the SRS withdrew from Italy.

POW rescue mission

On 28 May 1943, 2 SAS undertook Operation Snapdragon, the reconnaissance of the fortified island of Pantalleria. In Ops Chestnut and Narcissus 2 SAS attacked bridges and telephone communications and what was thought to be a fortified lighthouse with coastal artillery fire control equipment. Chestnut was a limited success, while the lighthouse proved to be deserted.

Two minor raids, Ops Marigold (30 May 1943) and Hawthorn (7 July 1943), were launched against Sardinia, and Jeep reconnaissance took 2 SAS via Taranto up to Termoli by October. As the German defences hardened along the Gustav line south of Rome, the Adriatic coast and mountainous interior became a 'target rich environment', to use the language of the Gulf War of 1990-91.

In September 1943, Ops Speedwell and Jonquil were launched. Jonquil was intended to collect Allied

PoWs who were at large in Italy, but proved to be a disaster, and few men were evacuated. Though Jonquil was not planned by the SAS, this did little to mitigate a feeling of frustration and disappointment. In contrast Speedwell, which used only two seven-man patrols, caused considerable disruption to rail links around the La Spezia/Genoa area.

In January 1944 a series of raids were launched to support the Allied landings at Anzio. In Op Pomegranate a team of six men from 2 SAS were parachuted into northern Italy to attack an airfield from which German reconnaissance aircraft were operating. It was the only airfield attack of the campaign; seven aircraft were attacked with Lewes bombs, but the force suffered casualties. In the same month in Op Baobab, a small group was landed on the Italian Adriatic coast to attack a bridge between Pesaro and Fano. Ops Maple and Driftwood were also directed against railway links and were a partial success. In March 1945, Op Tombola was one of the most successful SAS operations in Italy. Some fifty men from 3 Squadron 2 SAS under Major Roy Farran, with 70 escaped Russian PoWs and local Italian partisans, waged a war against German supply lines and the HQ at Albinea. By the end of the war the force had inflicted 600 casualties on the enemy and captured over 400.

SAS and D-Day

By January 1944 the Allied planners' attention was directed towards the landings in northern Europe. The SAS had expanded to a full brigade within the British 1st Airborne Corps. It was under command of Brigadier Roderick McLeod and was composed of 1 SAS (reconstituted from the SRS) under Lt Col 'Paddy' Mayne, 2 SAS under Will Stirling, two Free French parachute battalions (3 and 4 SAS) and an independent company of Belgian paratroops (5 SAS) (The modern Belgian Army has retained the SAS cap badge for their 1st Para-Commando Battalion which is worn with a maroon beret).

A squadron of 'phantom' signallers from GHQ Liaison Regiment were attached, as were Army supply and support services. As part of the 1st Airborne Corps, the men were ordered to wear their SAS cap badge on a maroon beret; many ignored the order.

The Army planners saw the role of the SAS as similar to that of the conventional airborne forces who were dropped to secure the flanks of the D-Day beaches. The SAS were to be used as a reconnaissance force ahead of the Allied tanks and motorised infantry – a role for which they had not trained and which would have produced very heavy casualties. William Stirling resigned in protest and the plans were changed;

101

command of 2 SAS passed to Lt Col Brian Franks.

SAS operations in France, like many of those in
Italy, were aimed at cutting or disrupting German
supply lines leading north to the Normandy
battlefields. Operations followed a proven procedure:
First an advanced party with a phantom signals
section was parachuted into the area to establish
contact with the Resistance. Then, when a good
dropping zone (DZ) had been located, the main part
arrived. Squadron-sized bases were established in
remote wooded areas, and through the summer of
1944 parachute drops of arms including mortars and
anti-tank guns, Jeeps, ammunition, explosives and
supplies were delivered to the SAS and local Maquis
by air drop.

The code names for operations reflected a distinctly
British character, part literary and part nostalgic for
London life. They ranged from the Wolsey and
Benson in the north near the Somme; through Defoe,
Titanic and Trueform in Normandy; Derry, Grog,
Dingson, and Cooney in Brittany; Gaff and Bunyan
near Paris; Haft near Mayenne; and Dunhill, Dickens,
Shakespeare, Chaucer, Gain and Spenser along the
Loire valley. Down the Rhone Saone valley operations
were Rupert, Loyton, Hardy, Newton, Barker and
Harrod, while in the Massif Central they were named
Haggard, Bulbasket, Moses, Jockworth, Samson,

Men of the French Forces of the Interior (FFI), the rather grand title given to the mixed groups of Resistants in France. Though the SAS worked with them, the Communist groups were aggressively independent and uncontrolled.

Snelgrove and Marshall. In Belgium, which offered far less cover than France, Caliban, Brutus and Bergbang were undertaken in the south east, while in the Netherlands the SAS launched Fabian and the uneuphonious Gobbo which had started life as Op Portia. In 1945 SAS operations in the Netherlands were Keystone, Amherst and Larkswood, while the final penetration into the hostile territory of the Third Reich were operations Howard and Archway.

Probably the most remarkable incident occurred on 23 August during Op Kipling near Auxerre. A Jeep patrol from C Squadron 1 SAS, under command of Capt David Harrison, heard reports that there were Germans in the village of Les Ormes. Entering it they found men and vehicles of a Waffen-SS unit and a firing party about to execute 20 civilians in reprisal for Resistance operations. The Jeeps roared into the village square and in savage cross fire an SAS trooper was killed and a Jeep destroyed, but 18 Frenchmen escaped.

Gestapo reprisals

However in Op Loyton in the Vosges, the men of 2 SAS under command of Lt Col Franks were pitted against large numbers of German soldiers with two Gestapo HQs at Nancy and Strasbourg which had dedicated anti-partisan units. Though the local Maquis were an unreliable ally, the villagers were co-operative and helpful and paid a heavy price. The 210 men and boys aged from 16 to 60 from the village of Moussey were deported to concentration camps, from which only 70 returned. When the SAS operation was terminated in October 1944, Lt Col Franks ordered his men to make their way to Allied lines. Of the 91

A plaque commemorates a parachutage to the French Resistance in the Department of Lot on July 14, 1944. The SAS were operating in the area before and after D-Day.

men who participated in Op Loyton two were killed and the 31 who were captured were murdered by the Gestapo.

Op Houndsworth by A Squadron 1 SAS, under the command of Major Bill Fraser, operated from the wooded hills west of Dijon. Attacks against the railway infrastructure with Maquis assistance derailed six trains, cut lines 22 times, destroyed 70 vehicles and caused 220 enemy casualties. In addition Houndsworth armed and trained around 300 Maquis. Their most successful coup was when the SAS ambushed a convoy containing men destined for deportation from the village of Montsauche. All the Germans were killed and the men escaped, but as a reprisal the Germans burned the village.

In Op Bulbasket Captain Tonkin from B Squadron 1 SAS demonstrated that direct action was not the only tactic to employ against the German forces in France. When he discovered that there were fuel tankers in the railway sidings at Chatelleraut, the information was passed back to the UK, and on 11 June an RAF raid destroyed the fuel that was destined for the 2nd Waffen-SS Panzer Division Das Reich which was moving north to Normandy.

Operations in Belgium were of a fairly short duration, many being overtaken by the speed of the Allied advance. Op Fabian in the Netherlands,

Two weapons containers parachuted to the Resistance in the Dordogne area in World War II , photographed in 1992.

conducted by men of the Belgian Independent Parachute Company (5 SAS) between September 1944 and March 1945, had been intended to gather intelligence on German V2 missile launching sites, but instead it became closely involved with the Dutch resistance assisting Allied paratroopers evading capture after the battle at Arnhem.

The operations in the Netherlands were aimed at capturing bridges and other key features to assist the Allied advance. Some, like Amherst undertaken by 3 and 4 French Parachute Battalions (3 and 4 SAS), were successful but costly. Though they killed 270 enemy, wounded 220 and took 187 prisoners, they suffered 29 killed and 35 wounded.

By May 1945 Germany was rapidly collapsing, but there was still stiff resistance to Ops Howard and Archway. The former, conducted by B and C Squadrons 1 SAS, was commanded by Lt Col 'Paddy' Mayne. Mayne won his fourth DSO extricating men from B Squadron who had been caught in an ambush. Archway had 430 men, 75 from two squadrons from 1 and 2 SAS, commanded by Lt Col Brian Franks. It was initially employed as a reconnaissance screen; then, pushing forward against rearguard actions by withdrawing German infantry, it reached Kiel on 3 May 1945.

Though the war had ended on 7-8 May 1945 there

Shoulder titles for 2nd and 4th SAS in the maroon colours of British airborne forces.

was still a 300,000 strong German garrison in Norway. Op Apostle was undertaken by HQ SAS Brigade and 1 and 2 SAS, all under command of Brigadier Mike Calvert. The brigade, based at Bergen with a strength of 845, disarmed and organised the repatriation of the Germans without any trouble.

SAS operations in North West Europe had been a success, but at a price. The Germans had suffered 2,000 killed, 7,733 wounded and 4,784 captured, and 18,000 had been persuaded to surrender. Some 700 vehicles and seven trains had been destroyed, 33 trains had been derailed, and tracks were cut on 164 separate occasions. In addition, target information as well as operational intelligence had been passed to the RAF. The SAS had suffered 330 casualties, and many French civilians and Maquis had been murdered by the Germans. Captured SAS, even though they were in recognised British uniform, were also murdered by Germans carrying out Hitler's Commando Order.

21 SAS Regiment (Artists)

With the end of the War the SAS, like many of the unconventional forces that had been developed, was disbanded. In 1947, however, the War Office gave the regiment a partial reprieve when it created an SAS regiment out of the long-established London based Territorial Army regiment, the Artists' Rifles. The 21 SAS Regiment (Artists) initially wore the old Mars and Minerva cap badge on a maroon beret, but soon reverted to the traditional SAS insignia.

On the other side of the world, Chinese Communists in Malaya had embarked on a campaign of subversion and terror in an attempt to impose a Communist regime on the federation of states which were soon to become independent. The insurgency drew on support from rural Chinese communities and had caused the death of over 1,300 policemen, soldiers and civilians.

Mars and Minerva, the cap badge of the Artists Rifles which became 21 SAS after World War II.

The Commander-in-Chief Land Forces, Far East, General Sir John Harding, asked Major Mike Calvert, a Chindit veteran and former commanding officer of the SAS Brigade in World War II, to analyse the situation. This Calvert did over six months on foot, alone and armed only with a rifle. His conclusion was that the Communist Terrorists (CTs) should be separated from the population by grouping isolated villages together in secure hamlets. This would deny the CTs food and recruits and the opportunity to conduct propaganda.

The second phase of the operation would be to send special forces patrols into the jungle to hunt down the CTs and deny them access to food and support from the indigenous aboriginal tribes. The patrols would win the 'hearts and minds' of the tribes with assistance and protection.

Calvert was given permission to recruit his 100-strong unit, which was named the A Squadron Malayan Scouts. It contained former Commandos, men from the SAS and an ad hoc counter-terrorist group called Ferret Force. B Squadron Malayan Scouts was formed from reservists from 21 SAS who had volunteered for service in Korea. C Squadron was recruited by Calvert while on a visit to Rhodesia.

A tough training programme was instituted near Johore and by the middle of 1951 the Malayan

Scouts were operational. Their tactics were to penetrate deep into the jungle, and establish a base which was re-supplied by air drops; patrols would then sweep the area.

When Calvert was invalided home in November 1951, command passed to Lt Col John 'Tod' Sloane who withdrew the Scouts from deep patrolling for re-organisation. Troublemakers in A Squadron were returned to unit (RTU'd — initials which carry terrible weight for soldiers in any special forces formation). D Squadron was raised by Major Dare Newell between 1951 and 1952.

When the Scouts returned to the jungle in 1952 they used an insertion technique called 'tree jumping'. Men were parachuted directly onto the top of the jungle canopy and would then rope down from the top of the trees using 30 metres of rope attached to their harness.

22 Regiment Special Air Service

In 1952 the Malayan Scouts became 22 Regiment Special Air Service, which meant ironically that 21 SAS, the Territorial Army regiment, was the origin of a Regular Army formation. Recruiting and selection in the UK was conducted by Major John Woodhouse, who would later return to Malaya to command a squadron.

113

Between 1952 and 1958 the standards for selecting officers, NCOs and troopers were raised. Some serving personnel were RTU'd to be replaced by a tough, intelligent and independent intake. NCOs included Sergeant Turnbull who was fluent in Malay and an expert tracker — in one operation he tracked a group of CTs for 14 weeks. He was awarded the Military Medal following an operation by 17 Troop D Squadron which killed four terrorist in the Perak-Kelantan area.

Among the new officers was a Light Infantry captain named Peter de la Billiere. He would later command 22 SAS and in 1990-91 lead British land forces in the Gulf War.

In December 1952 C Squadron returned to Rhodesia and was replaced by a New Zealand (NZ) squadron. About a third of the NZ squadron were Maoris, who established good relations with the shy Malayan aborigines. 'Hearts and minds' operations further helped win over the aborigines.

Fixed wing aircraft like Blackburn Beverleys dropped men and supplies, and patrols knew that wounded troopers could be evacuated by S51 helicopters.

Jungle skills developed fighting the Communist Terrorists (CTs) in the 1950s have been retained and form part of Continuation Training following Selection.

A Royal Marine reconnaissance patrol return from the jungle in Borneo during operations against the Indonesians in the early 1960s. The SAS conducted deep penetrations patrols into Indonesian territory to ambush road and river traffic and gain intelligence. The men in the photograph are armed with the Armalite rifle.

In the spring of 1958 the Malayan Emergency was almost over but D Squadron under Major H Thompson conducted a ten-day operation in stinking swamps near Telok Anson. Their target was two groups of CTs commanded by the notorious 'Baby Killer' Ah Hoi. Two troops were parachuted in and, after days immersed in water, found the camp. A cordon composed of the other two troops was put in place, but it took another ten days before the trap was sprung and ten CTs including Ah Hoi surrendered.

In six years of constant operations the SAS had killed 108 CTs. Compared to World War II these figures may seem a poor return, but patrolling, intelligence gathering and hearts and minds operations did as much to ensure the victory as confirmed kills.

From Jungle to Desert

Veterans say that soldiers and junior NCOs thrive in the jungle, where the tactics require quick reactions and involve short-range firefights, ambushes and

sniping. Officers prefer the desert where the visibility is generally good — they can co-ordinate mortars and artillery and observe the enemy over long ranges.

In November 1958 D Squadron went from jungle to desert, to the dry and rugged terrain of Jebel Akhdar in northern Oman. Jebel Akhdar is a 350 kilometre square plateau, with mountain peaks and narrow passes which were ideal for ambush.

British military assistance had been requested by the Sultan of Oman, whose rule had been challenged by Sulaiman bin Himyar, chief of the Bani Riyam tribe, the Imam, Ghalib bin Ali and his brother Talib. In 1957 Talib returned to Jebel Akhdar with an force of expatriate Omanis. He attracted support from two rebel tribes on the jebel: the Bani Himya and Bani Riyam. They were well armed and equipped and all came from a tradition where a man carries arms from adolescence, and is skilled in weapons handling and fieldcraft.

The 70 men of D Squadron under Major Johnny Watts arrived from Malaya in November 1958. They quickly went into action, and two groups under Capt

An FN-armed firquat in Dhofar in the early 1970s, pulls on his pipe. He has the characteristic dark green Omani shemagh, firquats with their local knowledge were an invaluable part of the 'hearts and minds' operations in Dhofar

Rory Walker took a feature nicknamed Sabrina and established sangars 2,000 metres from the enemy positions. A fierce attack against Walker's position was beaten off with heavy enemy losses.

To the south of the jebel Capt de la Billiere discovered a cave which contained arms and ammunition. He attempted to capture it, but his group was beaten off and forced to make a fighting withdrawal.

In January 1959 on the basis of air reconnaissance A Squadron, which had just arrived in Oman, was to make a joint assault with D. Their route would be from the south between two wadis and, though it was covered by an enemy light machine gun, a night approach combined with a deception plan would ensure surprise. A rumour was spread among the Arab donkey handlers that the axis of the attack would be from Tanuf in the west. The ruse worked and the enemy concentrated their strength there.

At 0300 on 26 January, A Squadron reached Sabrina from the north side of the jebel and secured the rebel position after a fierce firefight. The squadron, less 4 Troop which secured Sabrina, pushed south to Tanuf where it joined D Squadron at 1800. A diversionary attack was made from Tanuf at 2030. At the same time the two squadrons began their march up the jebel to their objectives of Pyramid, Vincent and Beercan (the summit).

An SAS OP covering a deep wadi in Oman watches for adoo movement.

By 0500 on the following day, with Vincent secure, D Squadron held Pyramid and was ready to assault Beercan. It was to be a steep climb and the men were instructed to reduce their loads to essential weapons and ammunition. After a gruelling 90-minute climb they reached the peak before sunrise. They had cracked open the rebel defences, which had included trenches and .50" heavy machine guns. Backed up by air strikes by the RAF against the rebels on the south side, the SAS cleared the remaining positions. They were consolidated by local Omani forces and dismounted troops of the Life Guards.

SAS operations in Borneo

When in 1962 a Federation of Malaysia was proposed, to incorporate Sabah, Sarawak and Brunei in Borneo and Malaya and Singapore on the mainland, President Sukarno of Indonesia saw it as a threat to his territorial ambitions and vowed to "smash Malaysia". He encouraged internal subversion by the Clandestine Communist Organisation (CCO), and as the Confrontation with Malaysia escalated sent regular forces across the border and even paratroops into the Malay peninsula.

A radio operator in the 1970s equipped with a PRC 316 checks details of a signal.

As part of its defence agreements with these former colonies, the British government and Commonwealth sent troops, including SAS squadrons, to contain the insurgency and external threat. Initially Major-General W Walker, the British commander in Borneo, planned to use the SAS as a mobile reserve that could be inserted by parachute to recapture villages seized by the Indonesians.

Lt Col John Woodhouse commanding 22 SAS persuaded him that the squadrons would be better used as a 'trip wire' along the 1,500 kilometre border providing intelligence about CCO and Indonesian movements. SAS patrols were deployed every 150km and immediately began a 'hearts and minds' programme with the local tribes: Dyaks, Muruts and Punans. Besides medical assistance to villages, one enterprising sergeant built a miniature hydro-electric plant, providing the only electric lighting for 600 kilometres.

The programme paid off as villagers grew to trust these men who lived with them, albeit in their own long house. The tribesmen were trained as irregular forces called Border Scouts and some moved freely over the border and were able to report Indonesian

Demolition training on a railway bridge , the belt order made with '44 Pattern water bottle carriers allowed kit to be carried comfortably.

troop movements. SAS patrols from A Squadron were relieved by D in 1963 which embarked on long operations deep along the estuaries of Sarawak's western frontier. One patrol from D Squadron stayed in the jungle in Long Jawi for six months.

In June 1964 the British government authorised Walker to launch top secret 'Claret' cross-border raids against Indonesian camps. Large scale attacks were undertaken by regular British infantry battalions, working on intelligence gathered by SAS patrols. However the SAS also ambushed river craft and enemy patrols.

B Squadron was reformed in January 1964; two years later G Squadron was formed from Guardsmen who had undertaken patrolling and close reconnaissance missions on the central Sarawak border as part of the Guards Independent Company. A and B Squadron conducted a number of Claret operations, in 1965 when D replaced A the operations continued.

Operations were extremely testing in a climate that sapped energy. Men living on cold rations, so that cooking smells would not be detected, returned from the jungle thin and pale. Patrolling in groups as small as two men, they moved at a slow pace to listen and observe at all times. Squadrons were rotated to allow men to recover and rebuild their strength.

Armed with an L4A4 Bren light machine gun an Australian soldier stands guard during an exercise in 1984. The Bren which had magazines compatible with the FN and SLR was a useful light automatic in the jungle and was used by British, Australian and New Zealand SAS.

In late May A Squadron, commanded by Major de la Billiere, replaced D and, working closely with the Gurkhas, initiated a series of cross-border raids.

In 1966 the Indonesian Army became disenchanted with Sukarno, his flirtation with the Communist party and the failed campaign against Malaysia. They

launched a coup d'etat and five months later
Indonesia ceased operations against Malaysia.

With the Emergency in Malaya and Confrontation
in Borneo the SAS had established jungle warfare as a
core skill. It is now part of the Continuation Training
phase for SAS personnel.

Aden and the Radfan

In the early 1960s Britain was in the process of
withdrawing from her colonial and protectorate
responsibilities east of Suez, and one of these was the
colony of Aden at the southern end of the Red Sea.
Egyptian and Soviet sponsored subversion as well as
rebellion by the mountain tribes in the Radfan put
pressure on the British government, which in 1964
assembled Radforce — composed of men of the 45
Cdo Royal Marines, 3rd Bn Parachute Regiment, 1st
Bn East Anglian Regiment, Royal Horse Artillery and
Aden's Federal Regular Army.

On the first operation 3 Troop A Squadron 22 SAS,
under Captain Robin Edwards, was tasked with
reconnoitring a possible Drop Zone (DZ) for
paratroops. However they were compromised and
during a gruelling 30 hours, supported by artillery fire

*A trooper prepares to windlass a dummy charge to a
girder on a bridge during a training exercise.*

and air strikes, they fought a running battle with hostile tribesmen. Though the patrol escaped during the night they were obliged to leave behind the bodies of Edwards and his signaller Warburton. The tribesmen decapitated them and the heads were exhibited in the Yemeni capital of Taiz. After this setback, SAS operations in the Radfan like OPs, and directing artillery and air strikes, settled into a routine. It was however a far harsher operational environment than Borneo.

In Aden town the 20 men from the SAS conducted counter-terrorist operations nick named 'Keeni Meeni' against the National Liberation Front (NLF) and the Front for the Liberation of South Yemen (FLOSY) (Keeni Meeni is a Swahili phrase which describes the sinuous movement of a snake). In the Crater and Sheikh Othman districts, the NLF and FLOSY had targeted British Special Branch officers and their informants, so Keeni Meeni patrols armed with 9mm Browning Hi-Power pistols and dressed as Arabs infiltrated the crowds. Some patrol members even went out in uniform as 'bait' for the assassins. The tactics worked, with the SAS scoring victories in fast, short range gun fights.

When Aden and Yemen became independent in 1967 and moved into the Soviet orbit as the People's Democratic Republic of Yemen (PDRY), the SAS

'Patrol Extraction' a painting of the Australian SAS in training. Formed after the War the Australian SAS saw action in Borneo and Vietnam.

could at least say that they had developed skills in urban counter-terrorism.

Operation Storm

Among the troopers and officers who fought in the campaign in Jebel Akhdar in 1958-59 was Lt Tony Jeapes who was with A Squadron. He would return to Oman 12 years later, first as a squadron commander and subsequently as CO of 22 SAS. He would play an important part in a campaign against rebel 'adoo' which lasted from 1970 to 1976, and which like the Confrontation would combine hearts and minds operations with ambushes, patrols and even set piece actions with artillery, air strikes and vehicles.

An insurgency in Jebel Dhofar by the Dhofar Liberation Front (DLF) against the reactionary Sultan Said bin Taimur, which begun in the 1960s, had been infiltrated by the radical People's Front for the Liberation of the Arabian Gulf (PFLOAG). PFLOAG was a communist organisation with cross-border backing from the PDRY as well as support from the USSR and China. By the late 1960s the PFLOAG controlled Dhofar and was posing a real threat to Oman and to the national interests of oil exporting countries along the Arabian Gulf and their customers, since Oman commands the sea-lane approaches to the area. In 1970 the Sultan was overthrown in a bloodless coup by his Sandhurst trained son Qaboos.

Qaboos immediately offered an amnesty to the adoo 'enemy' in Dhofar who wished to surrender, and began a programme of civil development in the area. The SAS Squadrons which were posted to Oman were described as a British Army Training Team (BATT) which meant that their operations could be described simply as 'training'. Lt Col Johnny Watts commanding 22 SAS identified 'Five Fronts' on which the SAS would have to fight if they were to win the campaign. They were: 1 Intelligence, 2 Information, 3 Medical, 4 Veterinary, 5 Enlisting

A Land Rover mounted SAS patrol in Oman , though the country has wide open classic desert, it also has deep wadis with thick scrub which were excellent cover for the adoo enemy.

Dhofaris. On these five fronts the SAS fought for six years. The first success came when a group of guerrillas under Salim Mubarak — who had become disenchanted by the atheist views and authoritarian manner of the PFLOAG — fought their way off the Jebel Dhofar and surrendered. Mubarak and Jeapes teamed up to propose to the British Brigadier and Sultan in the capital Salalah that these disenchanted former guerrillas be formed into firqats (companies)

133

of about 60 men. The former adoo traded their Soviet AK47 assault rifles for FN self loading rifles, and became skilled and dedicated fighters.

The SAS also initiated a civic affairs programme which included drilling new wells and re-opening the old ones that the former Sultan had ordered to be bricked up. Clinics cured many diseases which quickly responded to antibiotics, and also provided a place where low level intelligence could be gathered or passed on by men and women from the Jebel Dhofar.

Between September 1970 and March 1971, 200 adoo had returned to the government. Some of these men were experienced former soldiers from the Sultan's Armed Forces (SAF), including men who had attended training courses in the United Kingdom. They had been disenchanted with Said bin Taimur, but realised that under Qaboos the country was changing for the better.

A joint firqat and SAS operation recaptured the coastal town of Sudh on 24 February 1971. In October the 250 SAF, 100 SAS and five firqats launched Op Jaguar and established bases on the Jebel Dhofar. As the campaign developed a series of lines composed of barbed wire, mines, booby traps and ground sensors were constructed, anchored on the sea to the south and stretching between 50 and 75 kilometres northwards into the jebel. They prevented

PFLOAG forces taking the easy coastal infiltration route from the Republic of Yemen and forced then north into the mountains.

By the end of 1971 the SAS, with 700 Dhofaris fighting in firqats, were well established in the jebel and the hearts and minds programme was attracting more recruits to the firqats.

The Battle of Mirbat

The PFLOAG realised that they needed to score a substantial military victory for their own internal morale and to show that despite setbacks they were still winning. They decided to attack the small town of Mirbat, 65km east of Salalah. The attack was launched on 19 July 1972, when the adoo thought that seasonal rain and low cloud would prevent BAe Strikemasters from the Sultan of Oman's Air Force (SOAF) from operating. Some 250 AK47-armed adoo had infiltrated from jebel carrying an 84mm Carl Gustav anti-tank weapon and 75mm recoilless rifles.

Mirbat consisted of a cluster of houses and two forts: Wali Fort with a garrison of 30 North Omani Askaris, and the Gendarmerie fort on slightly higher ground with 25 Dhofar Gendarmes and a World War II vintage 25-pdr howitzer. Houses and forts were surrounded by a barbed wire fence. In addition to local forces, Mirbat had nine men from 8 Troop, B

Squadron, 22 SAS under command of 23-year-old Captain Mike Kealy. The SAS were in a building called the Batthouse with an 81mm mortar about 500 metres south west of the Gendarmerie Fort. A deception plan by the PFLOAG had drawn off a 60-strong firqat from Mirbat in pursuit of a group of adoo which had been spotted.

The attack began at 0500 when shots were fired at the adoo who were working their way towards the Gendarmerie fort. Trooper Labalaba began firing the 25-pdr and Corporals Pete Wignal and Roger Chapman engaged the enemy with a .50-in Browning and a 7.62mm General Purpose Machine Gun (GPMG). When Labalaba was wounded, Trooper Savesaki, a fellow Fijian, made a daring dash from the Batthouse to the fort with a first aid kit and the gun was kept in action.

The battle had been under way for two hours, with attacks on the Gendarmerie fort from the north and east and adoo in the wadi to the south. When radio communications with the fort ceased, Kealy with Trooper Tobin worked his way to the fort where he found Labalaba badly wounded but still manning the gun, and Savesaki with a back wound covering to the north. In the savage fighting that followed Kealy's arrival, Labalaba was hit again and died and Tobin was fatally wounded. At Kealy's request mortar fire was directed on the fort as the adoo were closing in.

Despite the poor weather two SOAF Strikemasters arrived to strafe the adoo from heights as low as 30 metres, to be followed by a second pair when their ammunition had been expended, and soon other troops in the town joined in the action. Twenty-three men of G Squadron had been lifted by helicopter to the shore south east of Mirbat and began to sweep northwards, driving the adoo away.

When the fighting was over Labalaba and Tobin were dead, and another two members of the Mirbat BATT were seriously wounded. On the battlefield were over 30 adoo dead. Kealy was awarded a DSO for his leadership in the battle. Tragically this talented soldier was to die of hypothermia in February 1979 during a long distance march on the Brecon Beacons.

Though the war was to last another four years, Mirbat marked the turning point. The hearts and minds work was passed to government agencies. In 1973, operating in conjunction with an Iranian Special Forces battalion, the SAS cleared the road through the jebel from Salalah and Thamrait, and a year later working with firqats the SAS cleared the adoo from central Dhofar. Though patrols, firefights and ambushes were a significant part of SAS operations in Oman, the hearts and minds work brought over more adoo to the Government than

137

A Rhodesian Alouette helicopter armed with a MAG. C Squadron the Rhodesian SAS used helicopters, aircraft, small boats and a variety of trucks to conduct internal and cross border operations during the war in Rhodesia.

firefights killed, and reformed adoo who joined firqats were twice as valuable as efficient soldiers and emissaries to the interior tribes.

Counter-Revolutionary Warfare

The Keeni Meeni operations in Aden in 1967 were a pointer to a new role for the SAS which was to develop in the early 1970s. The threat to Western democracies from terrorist groups, many of which had sponsors in Communist Eastern Europe or the Soviet Union, had grown since the late 1960s. In September 1972, 11 Israeli Olympic athletes died along with their Palestinian kidnappers when the German police bungled the attempt to save them. The photographs of burned out UH1 helicopters at Munich airport were a mute testimony to the way that even in death, a fanatical terrorist group could seize headlines.

After Munich, West Germany set in motion a programme to train a Federal Counter Terrorist organisation which was given the innocuous name Grenzschutzgruppe 9 (GSG9), or Border Group 9.

In Hereford, the home of 22 SAS Regiment, ideas about a counter-terrorist role had already been mooted, but Munich gave them new impetus. A Counter Revolutionary War (CRW) wing had been set up in 1972 and at the end of the year the 20 strong 'Pagoda' Squadron, the CRW team under command of Lt Col Anthony Pearson, became operational. It had three roles: collecting intelligence on terrorist threats, pre-empting terrorist activity, and conducting direct action against terrorist operations. Direct action included hostage rescue from buildings, aircraft, ships, oil-rigs and even nuclear power stations.

For this work the squadron had a range of

*The African bush offered ample opportunities for
ambush for Rhodesian and ZIPRA and ZANLA forces.*

sophisticated portable communications, surveillance
and monitoring equipment. Training exercises with
the Home Office and regional police forces developed
good working relationships as well as giving Pagoda
Squadron access to a range of possible targets. Cross-
training and assistance from counter-terrorist forces
like French GIGN, US Delta Force and Dutch
Special Border Police, as well as assistance during
operations, helped to build up an international force
against terrorism.

Balcombe Street Siege

The first operation for which Pagoda Squadron was
activated — a hijack at Stansted in 1975 — ended
peacefully. Later that year the SAS were deployed to
central London, where a four-man IRA Active Service
Unit (ASU) had holed up in a flat in Balcombe Street
after an attack on a restaurant. In the flat they held
the owners, a middle aged couple, hostage. The siege
by the Metropolitan Police lasted eight days, and
radio and newspaper reports stated that an SAS team
had been deployed, including snipers. The ASU had
been monitoring outside news on a radio set in the
flat and decided that faced with possible death in an

SAS assault, surrender and jail was a preferable prospect.

In May 1977 members of the Squadron were present when the Dutch authorities were confronted by a train hijack by South Moluccan terrorists.

Hijack at Mogadishu

In October that year two members of the squadron, Maj Alastair Morrison and Sgt Barry Davis, were of direct assistance to a 26-strong GSG9 team under Ulrich Wegener. A Lufthansa Boeing 737 with 86 passengers and five crew had been hijacked by a German/Palestinian terrorist cell. After a tortuous flight around the Gulf states it had arrived at Mogadishu in Somalia, followed by a Lufthansa aircraft with German negotiators and the GSG9 team. The two SAS men not only had excellent contacts throughout the Gulf and so could advise GSG9 on local assistance, but carried with them 'stun grenades'.

At Mogadishu the stun grenades were detonated as a diversion outside the aircraft as the GSG9 team stormed in. Three of the four terrorists were killed and only four passengers were slightly injured. Operation Fire Magic, as GSG9 had codenamed the operation, had been successfully concluded.

The SAS had, as is their practice, managed to keep a

The Heckler and Koch MP5A3 sub-machine gun which is a very reliable 9mm weapon with a high rate of fire. It was adopted by the SAS and numerous other special forces world-wide.

low profile during the Mogadishu and Balcombe Street operations, even though the UK media made some intelligent — and some less intelligent — guesses at their role. But in May 1980, the Counter Revolutionary Warfare team found itself filmed in action on prime time television and splashed across the front pages of even the most sober broadsheet newspapers.

The SAS action at the Iranian Embassy at Princess Gate London, the team moves across the roof prior to abseiling down to get access through the windows.

Storming the Embassy

On the morning of 30 April 1980, six Iraqi-sponsored terrorists who were members of the Democratic Revolutionary Front for the Liberation of Arabistan (an area of west Iran close to the Iraqi border) entered the Iranian Embassy. They took 26 hostages from the Embassy staff, a BBC journalist and PC Trevor Lock from Scotland Yard's Diplomatic Protection Group who had been on duty at the Embassy. There was a

Moments before entering the windows one of the team becomes entangled in his ropes.

A simultaneous assault is launched at the front of the building with a frame charge which the team use to blast their way through the windows.

bitter irony that at the same time in Tehran, US Embassy staff were being held hostage by Iranian Revolutionary Guards. Op Eagle Claw, the attempt by the US Delta Force to release them, would lead to the debacle at the airfield at Desert One.

Soon after the take-over of the Iranian Embassy at Princess Gate, the building was surrounded by specialist police units including D11 police

On the road outside other members of the team provide cover and radio communications.

marksmen, C13 anti-terrorist officers, members of the Special Patrol Group (SPG) and C7, Scotland Yard's Technical Support Group. The terrorists demanded the release of 91 Arabs held in Iranian jails and their transfer to Britain. The negotiations were to be conducted by Arab ambassadors in London. The terrorists set a deadline of mid-day on 1 May, otherwise they would start killing the hostages and destroy the building.

147

Police negotiators persuaded them to drop the demand for the release of prisoners, but the terrorists demanded that their request for mediators be broadcast. It was and had no effect.

The Prime Minister, Margaret Thatcher, brought together COBRA, the Cabinet Office Briefing Room which included members of the Ministry of Defence (MoD), MI5, MI6, and the SAS. Their recommendations were passed on to the Joint Operations Centre (JOC) at MoD. The UK media had moved into place outside the embassy, even erecting scaffolding platforms for TV cameras.

At the barracks at Regents Park, the SAS soldiers were building up a picture of the embassy from intelligence from C7 which had used microphones, thermal imagers and other surveillance devices to discover which rooms were occupied. Like all good plans, the SAS's proposed operation was simple. A four-man team would abseil from the roof down the rear of the building, while another team would enter the first floor by crossing the adjoining balcony. Frame charges would be used to blast through the windows, stun and CS grenades would be lobbed in, and the teams would enter. The team members wore black one-piece overalls, a colour selected because it showed more clearly in a smoky or CS filled room — and also because a black-clad man in a S6 respirator

The aftermath inside the embassy.

has a considerable psychological impact. They wore
fragmentation jackets (flak jackets) and carried 9mm
Browning Hi-Power pistols or Heckler & Koch MP5
sub-machine guns.

On the morning of 5 May there were indications
that the situation in the Embassy was beginning to
deteriorate. At 1850hrs a shot was heard and the body
of the Iranian press officer was dumped on the steps
outside the building. The negotiations took on new
urgency — but as the police were talking to the
terrorists over the telephone, responsibility for
operations at the Embassy was being formally passed

in writing at 2000hrs from the Metropolitan Police Deputy Assistant Commissioner John Dellow to Lt Col Michael Rose commanding 22 SAS. Op Nimrod had begun.

The assault by the group at the front went smoothly and was caught on live TV. At the back of the building one of the abseiling troopers had become entangled, so instead of using frame charges, the men sledge-hammered the windows open. The leader of the terrorist group was killed on the first floor and the SAS troopers made their way quickly to the telex room on the second floor where through C7 intelligence they knew that the hostages were being held.

Here the terrorists started firing, killing one hostage and wounding two others. The SAS burst in, killing two terrorists and capturing one. The young surviving terrorist had been shielded by women hostages. Two more terrorists died in the hallway and at the back of the building. In 17 minutes Op Nimrod was over as the hostages were bundled out of the building, which had started to burn following the detonation of stun and CS grenades. The SAS, who had suffered no casualties, left in two vans. Afterwards it is reported that at No 10 Downing Street they watched recordings of the TV coverage of the operation. A year later a coroner's inquest recorded a verdict of justifiable killing.

The team secure hostages with plasticuffs and evacuate them from the building.

151

SAS soldiers saw further action in the 1980s in Gambia, rescuing the family of the President Sir Dawda Jawara during an attempted coup d'etat in July 1981. In 1987 they rescued a prison officer held hostage in a five-day riot in Peterhead Prison, Aberdeen, in an operation which saw the use of stun and CS grenades, but which produced no casualties.

SAS against the IRA

The 'Troubles' in Northern Ireland, as the local population describe the murders, ambushes and intimidation and resulting high level of police and military activity, began in the late 1960s as a civil rights movement for the minority Catholic community. This was mishandled by elements of the local police, and sectarian riots in Londonderry and later Belfast led to the deployment of the British Army in 1969.

Initially the Army was welcome in the Catholic areas as a neutral force, but this did not last long. Sadly some heavy-handed tactics by the Army, which culminated in 1972 with 'Bloody Sunday' in Londonderry when men of the Parachute Regiment fired on a Civil Rights march killing 13, convinced the Catholic community that the Army was a new enemy. Interestingly, during the 'honeymoon' phase D Squadron 22 SAS assisted, patrolling in uniform wearing regimental berets and cap badges.

Water tanks filled with concrete block a minor road on the Irish border with Ulster. Despite these precautions the border has always been permeable.

In 1970 the Provisional Irish Republican Army (PIRA), which had broken away from the IRA, became active with a Marxist political agenda which included the unification of the North with the Republic of Eire. The IRA (as PIRA later became known) dominated the Catholic areas of West Belfast and large areas of Londonderry as well as the borders including South Armagh.

A separate terrorist organisation, the Irish Nationalist

153

Liberation Army (INLA), split away from the IRA but conducted operations similar in character. The Troubles have changed over the years from the urban riots of the 1970s, to sniping and bombing, and extortion, robbery and 'protection' which provided funds for both Loyalist and Nationalist terrorist groups. Though both Loyalists and Nationalists had political agendas, both groups also contained a small number of murderous psychopaths and criminals.

The end of the war in Dhofar released larger numbers of SAS soldiers for operations in Northern Ireland. The spur for their deployment came in 1976 after the IRA murdered 11 Protestants in a bus in South Armagh and killed three soldiers in their covert observation post (OP). The British Government announced that the SAS would be sent to Northern Ireland, and D Squadron based at Bessbrook Mill began operations. Much of their work involved long term covert OPs observing the movements of known IRA suspects and their associates. Between 1976 and 1989 it is asserted that 37 IRA and INLA terrorists have died in gun battles with the SAS, while the Regiment has lost four men: L Cpl David Jones, Capt Richard Westmacott, Sgt Paul Oram and L Cpl Alistair Slater.

Capt Westmacott died on 2 May 1980 when eight men in a two-car patrol were directed to 371 Antrim

SAS AGAINST THE IRA

The view from the watch tower in a permanent vehicle check point (PVCP) close to the Irish border photographed in the mid 1980s in Northern Ireland. Even PVCPs provided background on terrorist movements.

155

Road, Belfast, where suspicious activity had been reported. As soon as the cars pulled up — one at the back and one at the front — the car at the front came under fire from an IRA M60 machine gun which killed Westmacott instantly. The SAS believed the fire had come from number 369 which they attacked and cleared. Fortunately the Royal Ulster Constabulary (RUC) had sealed off the area when the shooting started and the terrorists were persuaded to surrender. In later years the SAS would favour a more patient approach with surveillance rather than direct action.

It is not Army policy to say whether an operation has been carried out by the SAS or special units of the Army or the RUC. Indeed the SAS are often happier when successful ambushes are attributed to the RUC or routine Army patrols.

In March 1976 a team 'lifted' a known IRA man, Sean McKenna, from his home in the Irish Republic and passed him on to an Army patrol; other raids brought in Kevin Byrne and Patrick Mooney. In April 1976 a four-man team snatched another suspect, Sean Cleary, from his fiancée's home near Forkhill, South Armagh. While they were waiting for a helicopter Cleary tried to break free and was killed in the struggle. This prompted accusations from the Nationalist community that the SAS were operating as a 'hit squad'.

Arrested by the Garda

The border with the Republic is not clearly defined and in May 1976 an eight man patrol was arrested by the Garda when they strayed across. They were charged with possessing unlicensed weapons and appeared in a closed court in Dublin where they were fined. By the late 1970s the British Army had deployed a new specialist force in Northern Ireland designated 14 Intelligence and Security Company, or Intelligence and Security Group (Northern Ireland). Training in some techniques had been undertaken by the SAS and thereafter it was difficult to distinguish between operations by both organisations. Ironically in September 1989 men from 14 Int and Security arrested a Loyalist gunman who had just attempted to assassinate the Sinn Fein leader Gerry Adams.

The SAS had been involved in surveillance and numerous small scale ambush operations against the IRA in the 1980s. In the spring of 1987 information was received that two IRA Active Service Units (ASUs) from East Tyrone were planning an attack on an RUC station at Loughall in North Armagh. The attack would use an wheeled digger with an explosive charge in the bucket to ram and blast its way into the station.

Aftermath of 'Operation Judy': the bullet-riddled IRA van

Ambush at Loughall

A large scale ambush operation code named 'Judy' was set in motion by the RUC, SAS and the Army. On 8 May the ASUs launched their attack: three men on a JCB with its bomb and eight men following in a stolen Toyota van. At 1920hrs the JCB crashed through the perimeter wall while the occupants of the van dressed in blue boilersuits sprayed the building with automatic fire. As the JCB crew ran back to the van to escape, the ambush was sprung. Four men died

The effects of the IRA bomb on the police station

in the van and four were killed in the open. After clearing the immediate area the SAS team was lifted out and an Army and RUC cordon established around the area. Tragically two innocent civilians in a white Citroen which had followed the Toyota had been caught in the fire from the ambush cut-offs; one was killed and the other badly wounded.

At the end of the year the IRA attacked a Remembrance Day service at Enniskillen, killing numerous worshippers and civilians. They needed a 'military victory' and looked abroad.

The perimeter defences were breached by a stolen JCB containing the bomb

Stopping the bombers

In 1988 an ASU composed of Daniel McCann, Sean Savage and Mairead Farrell travelled to Spain with the intention of detonating a car bomb outside the Governor's residence as the Band and Guard of the 1st Bn The Royal Anglian Regiment changed guard. Both the British and Spanish intelligence services were aware that an attack was imminent. On 6 March the ASU crossed from Spain into Gibraltar, and Savage parked a car close to the Governor's Residence. The group split up and moved on foot towards the Spanish border, followed by men of a SAS Special Projects Team who had been flown into Gibraltar.

The intelligence services assumed that the ASU would be armed, and would detonate the car bomb by a radio signal. In fact they were not armed, and planned to use a time delay on the bomb. The car that they had parked was a 'blocker' — an empty vehicle which would be moved at the last moment and replaced by the car bomb. This vehicle was found later in Spain by the Spanish Police. It was packed with 60kg of Semtex plastic explosives.

The ASU split up, but when at 1600hrs a Gibraltar Police car turned on its siren and made a U turn in the road, the ASU reacted violently. The men from the Special Projects Team, assuming they were armed and prepared to detonate the bomb, opened fire. All three were killed, but the controversy that followed, including a highly publicised Coroner's Inquest, helped to foster an image promoted by the IRA that the SAS were 'licensed to kill'.

On 3 June 1991 three IRA men were killed in the main street of Coagh, County Tyrone, when their Vauxhall Cavalier was fired on by soldiers from a 'specialist covert army operations' organisation, which many believed to be the SAS. The car was hit by 200 rounds and Peter Ryan, Lawrence McNally and Tony Dorris, all known terrorists, were killed.

SAS & SBS in the Falklands

In April 1982, hoping to boost the popularity of his military government, General Leopoldo Galtieri capitalised on the landings on South Georgia by Argentine scrap merchants and ordered the invasion of the Falkland Islands and the military occupation of South Georgia. Sovereignty over the Falklands, known to Argentina as the Malvinas, has been long disputed, but the English-speaking population have always expressed the wish to remain British. After a short resistance the Royal Marine garrison NP 8901 was obliged to surrender, and Argentina occupied the islands.

The sea, air and land operation to recover them,

The Royal Navy bombards South Georgia during Operation Paraquat in 1982. Op Paraquat was the joint SAS and Royal Marine attack on the island, which liberated it with a minimum of casualties on both sides.

codenamed Corporate, included several classic actions by the SAS and the Royal Marines Special Boat Squadron (SBS). In 1982 the SAS Group was commanded by Brigadier Peter de la Billiere, and 22 SAS by Lt Col Michael Rose. They committed D and G Squadron and the Regimental HQ.

Before attempting the Falklands it was decided that South Georgia, 1,200km to the east, should be secured. In an operation codenamed Paraquat, a party composed of men from the SAS, No 2 Section SBS and M Coy 42 Commando Royal Marines, under command of Major Cedric Delves, landed by boat and helicopter on the bleak island. Reconnaissance teams which had landed on Fortuna Glacier on 22 April were withdrawn because the weather was too severe, but men from Boat Troop landed and set up OPs.

On April 25, after Royal Navy helicopters had strafed and disabled the Argentine submarine Santa Fe at Grytviken harbour in South Georgia, Major Delves took his little force — 75 men in three groups — and landed them by helicopter. Bluff and naval gunfire induced the Argentine garrison of 100 at Grytviken to surrender, followed a day later by a smaller force at Leith.

Patrols had been landed on the Falklands from the beginning of May to establish the strength and location of the Argentine garrison and assess where would be the most secure site for an amphibious operation. Operations were concentrated around Bluff Cove, Stanley, Berkeley Sound, Cow Bay, Port Salvador, San Carlos Water, Goose Green on West

A Royal Artillery officer examines a dress sword captured at Fanning Head the Argentine position which dominated the approaches to San Carlos and which was attacked by the SBS prior to the main landings.

Falkland, Port Howard, Fox Bay and on Pebble Island. They built up a picture of the routine and location of the 11,000-strong garrison, and the location of its 42 fixed wing aircraft and helicopters. Information was formatted into alpha numeric codes and then passed by radio using 'burst transmission' which lasted a few seconds and therefore could not be located by DFs — electronic Direction Finding equipment. The men stayed in position for periods of 26 days or more, some almost under the enemy's noses.

Tragically a hide near Port Howard was discovered on 10 June and attacked. Captain John Hamilton of D Squadron was killed as he covered the escape of his signaller, who was later captured. The Argentine officer who led the assault asserted that Capt Hamilton deserved a posthumous VC; he received a posthumous MC. Capt Hamilton had played an important part in the recapture of South Georgia and the action at Pebble Island.

Pebble Island Raid

Pebble Island was almost a re-play of the SAS in its early days in North Africa. The grass airstrip on Pebble Island, at the northern end of West Falkland, had six Pucara ground attack aircraft, four Turbo-Mentors and a Shorts Skyvan which would be within

An old but classic picture of the SBS in training. The silenced Sterling sub-machine gun was also used by Argentine special forces during their landings on the Falklands

a short flight of the proposed Task Force landing site at San Carlos.

On the night of 14 May, 45 men of D Squadron were flown in by helicopter from HMS Hermes and met by a member of Boat Troop. The party was split into three: Mountain Troop would attack the aircraft, while the other two troops covered the approaches.

The attack on the airstrip was led by John

167

Hamilton, and was supported by naval gunfire from HMS Glamorgan. The party destroyed the aircraft with explosives, cratered the strip and blew up an ammunition dump. The Argentine garrison had been totally surprised and were only able to return inaccurate fire which wounded one member of the raiding party.

On 19 May tragedy struck when a Sea King helicopter took off from HMS Hermes to transfer men to the assault ship HMS Intrepid. In the darkness the helicopter was hit by a large sea bird which caused it to ditch from engine failure. Of the men on board, 18 from D squadron died in the bitterly cold Atlantic.

The SAS raided Darwin as part of a diversionary action during the main landings at San Carlos. On their return they shot down a Pucara with a FIM-92A Stinger SAM. This was the first time the Stinger had been used in action by the SAS.

Following the landings the SAS and SBS conducted deep penetration patrols, and on the night of 30 May the SAS assisted 42 Commando in the capture of Mount Kent. A journalist watching the SAS at de-briefs after these patrols noted that, though the Royal Marines and Parachute Regiment used bravura language like 'slotting' or 'zapping', the SAS would simply report after a contact that they had killed or

A damaged Scout helicopter is lifted away from HQ 3 Commando Brigade close to Stanley following an Argentine air attack on June 13, 1982. The 3 Cdo Bde used the Mountain and Arctic Warfare Cadre for long range patrolling and reconnaissance in a special forces role.

wounded the enemy.

A final raid on Stanley harbour was carried out on June 13 by a combined SAS, SBS and Royal Marine party headed by Major Delves. This was intended to be a diversion during the 2 Para attack on Wireless Ridge, but it was discovered and came under heavy fire. The party was obliged to scatter and was later picked up by helicopter.

While these operations were under way, the

An SAS patrol exits from a Scout helicopter at Bluff Cove following an extraction. The rather elderly Scout was a robust aircraft capable of lifting a patrol and its equipment.

commanding officer, Lt Col Mike Rose, had directed a subtle psychological warfare operation against the Argentine garrison. With Captain Rob Bell, a Spanish speaking Royal Marine, he had sent daily messages on the open radio net explaining the worsening military situation and urging that the Argentine garrison should talk. On 14 June an Argentine officer came on the net, and at his request Rose and Bell flew into Stanley and began the surrender negotiations. The

Argentine commander-in-chief General Menendez with his staff met Colonel Rose, Captain Bell and General Jeremy Moore commanding the British land forces.

Outside an SAS signaller was in contact with the satellite link to the Prime Minister. The negotiations ensured that a surrender would take place "with dignity and honour". West Falkland was surrendered without a fight, saving Argentine and British lives.

Special Forces in the Gulf War

The invasion of Kuwait by the Iraqis on 2 August 1990 gave the Iraqi leader Saddam Hussein control over a respectable proportion of the world's oil resources. His actions threatened Saudi Arabia, the key oil producer in the Middle East, and these moves prompted the US President George Bush to initiate Op Desert Shield.

The bulk of the men, women and resources for Desert Shield, and for Desert Storm which followed, came from the United States, but Britain contributed an armoured Division and men from 22 SAS. The joint British Commander in Chief in the Gulf was an old friend and veteran of the SAS, General Sir Peter de la Billiere. His wisdom and knowledge of the potential of Special Forces was essential in convincing General Norman Schwarzkopf, who commanded the

General Sir Peter de la Billiere at the cease fire negotiations in Iraq following the end of the ground war. 'DLB' is wearing the unique SAS beige beret reflecting his lifetime with the SAS.

Coalition ground forces, that they had a valuable role.
   Patrols were inserted into Iraq overland and by air, and were tasked with a variety of missions. Coalition planners in Riyadh wanted to know if the ground in Iraq would support tanks and heavy vehicles, so samples were required. The Iraqi communications network which used buried fibre optic cables was invulnerable to air attack, but could easily be cut with explosive charges placed by hand. Iraqi chemical or nuclear installations and communications centres deep in the desert were of interest to the planners,

A close up of the massive destruction to a HAS caused by a cluster of LGBs hitting one point.

Hardened Aircraft Shelters (HAS) in Kuwait destroyed by Coalition laser guided bombs (LGBs). Special forces equipped with laser designators can direct LGBs onto targets with a very high level of accuracy.

and once they had been identified could be designated for GBU-15 and GBU-10 Paveway II laser-guided bombs.

A close liaison developed between SAS patrols and the US Air Force Fairchild A10 Thunderbolt II or 'Wart Hog' ground attack aircraft. The heavily armoured, slow flying A10s were equipped with bombs, missiles and a powerful nose mounted GAU-8/A 30mm cannon which could pulverise enemy tanks and AFVs.

When the air war began Saddam Hussein reasoned

A two seat Fast Attack Vehicle armed with a Browning .50 and GPMG leaves the ground during a mobility demonstration. FAVs were used in the Gulf in 1991 by US special forces.

that if he could provoke Israel into attacking, this would destroy the fragile Coalition which included Syria and Egypt, as well as Saudi Arabia and forces from Kuwait which had managed to escape across the border. He therefore ordered that SCUD surface to surface missiles with HE warheads be launched against Israel. The fear in Israel and Saudi Arabia was that these missiles might have chemical warheads, notably nerve agents like GB or Sarin, which he had used against the Iranians.

To ensure that Israel stayed out of the war, the SAS

A patrol equipped with Milan anti-tank guided weapons deploys from a Puma. Anti-tank missiles give special forces a stand off capability with which they can engage key points.

and US Special Forces were tasked with Scud hunting. Scuds and their transporters were identified and Coalition aircraft directed onto them. Direct attack with Land Rover mounted anti-tank missiles and machine guns was also undertaken.

An RAF Puma medium lift helicopter takes off against a classic desert back ground. Iraq had wadis which offered cover to SAS patrols which had been inserted at night by helicopter.

The veteran Browning .50 heavy machine gun fitted with laser range finder on a ground mount. The Browning "five O" has been fitted to Jeeps and light vehicles by US, British and French special forces from World War II to the 1990s.

After the war ended, the SAS found their operations written up in lurid accounts which included men disguised as Iraqis chatting in Arabic in the middle of Baghdad. In fact the soldiers had been issued with locally made long sheepskin coats as a protection against the bitter Iraqi winter. Men wore goggles and shemaghs, the practical Arab head-dress, wrapped around their faces and on more than one occasion a vehicle mounted patrol miles from the Saudi border

The Harley Davidson military motorcycle can be carried attached to the rear of a 3/4 ton Land Rover and allows the crew to reconnoitre forward from a hide. It was used by the SAS in Iraq during the Gulf War.

had been mistaken for Iraqi soldiers.

SAS in the 21st Century

The end of the Cold War and with it the end of Communist sponsorship of terrorist organisations and insurgency, as well as the threat of a European land battle between NATO and the Warsaw Pact, changed the character and role of Special Forces. The

179

A sniper in Australia fires a bore-aligned Small Arms Weapons Effects Simulator (SAWES) at a distant target.

Volunteer Regiments, 21 and 23 had trained as 'stay behind' OPs, digging in and living like moles in hides as Warsaw Pact forces rolled over them. They would then emerge and, using secure radio communications, pass back to NATO forces details of the equipment and vehicles they could observe.

The IRA Ceasefire in Northern Ireland led to a reduction of the Army garrison and its presence on the streets. The Special Forces, while retaining vigilance, also reduced their level of activity. There are reports that 22 SAS has taken over the close

The GPMG in the light role with a Pilkington Optronics Super Kite Image Intensifying night sight. The Super Kite is a commercial development of the Common Weapons Sight (CWS) used by the British Army and special forces.

A Wessex Saker 400 kg light strike vehicle showing the crew positions. It has been suggested that special forces could use similar vehicles to conduct raids with a 4 tonne truck as a base vehicle.

protection of senior officers and VIPs from the Royal Military Police.

In Bosnia during the United Nations deployment, the use of air power was hedged about with caveats and controls. When General Sir Michael Rose and subsequently General Sir Rupert Smith requested air strikes, it is reported that these were laser designated

A Soviet Luna-M surface-to-surface missile (SSM) mounted on its ZIL-1325 transporter erector. Iraq had developed its own SSMs from Soviet missiles and these became an important target for British and American special forces in Iraq.

Soldiers with a 7.62mm General Purpose Machine Gun (GPMG) in a sustained fire role. The SAS first employed the GPMG in Oman in the 1970s where its fire power startled the adoo.

A sniper uses his telescope to observe a distant target. His camouflaged outfit made from strips of hessian and netting makes him almost invisible when his is prone in his hide. The weapon is a 7.62mm Accuracy International L96A1 bolt action rifle.

by SAS teams. It is hard to predict the character of future conflicts or the nature of terrorism that Britain may face, but whatever form they take, there will always be a role for the SAS.

The Cold War and Beyond

Chapter 3: The Cold War and Beyond

Immediately after 1945 there was a move in the British Army to get back to 'Real Soldiering' as one pre-War regular put it. This meant that 'private armies' like the SAS, LRDG, Army Commandos and PPA were disbanded. The Royal Marines kept the Commando raiding skills alive and have adopted the title. Currently there are three Commandos – 40 Cdo, 42 Cdo and 45 Cdo.

It was the Malayan Emergency of 1948-57 that demonstrated a continuing need for Special Forces. During the Korean War of 1950-53 reconnaissance and patrol units were formed, albeit on a unit level.

During the Mau Mau revolt in Kenya from 1952 to 1960 Major Frank Kitson discovered that like captured spies, surrendered guerrillas could be 'turned'. His counter-gangs of reformed terrorists knew how their former comrades operated and were of considerable value in the battle against a cruel tribal insurgency. The counter-gangs anticipated the role of the firqats of the Oman war in the 1970s.

The Green Berets

As Special Forces developed after World War II, their role fell into three areas. The first was conventional war, in which they would be used for long range reconnaissance and intelligence gathering, and direct attack against high priority targets. The threat of

The insignia of the US Army Special Warfare Center based at Fort Bragg North Carolina. Its design prompted comments about cooking pots but the Center enjoyed the patronage of President Kennedy.

189

conventional war in Europe lasted from the 1950s to 1989, when Communism and the Warsaw Pact collapsed. The second was counter-insurgency, which involved assisting friendly governments under threat from Communist-sponsored rebels. This was spurred by the take-over of Cuba by Fidel Castro and his export of Communism to Latin America, which lasted from the 1950s to the late 70s. The final role is counter-terrorism and hostage rescue. Terrorism came to the fore in the 1970s and 80s and is still a threat. It is driven by religion, nationalism and also by the huge sums of money generated by the illegal drugs trade.

In Europe in the early 60s the US Army saw a role as advisers and training staff for irregular forces which would spring up following a Soviet invasion. The United States had many emigres who had grown up in countries like Czechoslovakia, Hungary and Poland, and not only spoke English and their original native language, but had a strong hatred of the Communist government of their old homes. The US Army Special Forces, better known as Green Berets, were established in 1952 with this European role. In 1961 their operational philosophy was formalised in the manual FM 31-21 'Guerrilla Warfare and Special Forces Operations'. In the same year FM 31-15 'Operations Against Irregular Forces' was published. The two manuals encapsulate the role of the Green Berets:

The insignia of the Green Berets or US Army Special Forces which had begun as a small elite but expanded during the Vietnam War. The patch was known as the 'Saigon Electrical Works' badge.

A slightly theatrical picture of the Land Rover Special Operations Vehicle or SOV, it is based on the 110 model and has a strong roll bar frame. Land Rovers are favoured by US special forces because they are more compact than the HMMWV.

1. To seek out, train and support men capable of becoming effective guerrillas, and

2. To seek out, engage, and neutralize guerrillas.

In the Vietnam War the Green Berets were actively engaged in the counter-guerrilla role. However their training included 'Hearts and Minds' work like advice and assistance in farming and health and hygiene.

During the early years of the Vietnam War the Green Berets had a higher public profile than in retrospect they would have liked. The beret, though widely worn by European armies, had not previously been worn in the US Army. The philosophy of the Green Berets had an enthusiastic sponsor in President John F Kennedy whose challenge "Ask not what my country can do for me, but what I can do for my country" was a rallying call for the United States. After his assassination and burial at Arlington Cemetery in 1963, a green beret was among the

The Swedish AT4 anti-tank weapon adopted by the US Army was first used in action by special forces during Operation Just Cause in Panama.

Among a litter of ALICE packs and water containers two men of the 82nd Airborne keep watch in Grenada. Though special forces may use different equipment, they often make an effort to conform to a standard military appearance in order not to attract attention.

wreaths and tributes placed at the eternal flame. In a world that had been dominated by the threat of a nuclear exchange, which would make any human endeavour meaningless, or by massive armoured assaults across Europe, Special Forces whose equipment and skills were summed up as "A rifle, a bergen and a beret" challenged the military pessimists.

A member of the 1st Battalion, 7th Special Forces Group, Fort Bragg teaches the operating principles of the M79 grenade launcher to Salvadorian troops in1983.

The Special Forces mystique made as many enemies as it attracted good men. However the standards were, and still are, high. Entry qualifications require soldiers to be jump qualified, a high school graduate, and to have passed Basic Training, Advanced Individual Training, the Advanced Physical Readiness Test and the junior NCOs' course, and to be able to swim 50 metres in boots and uniform. Each man is security vetted.

There is a Selection and Post-Selection phase. Selection begins with a three-week phase which includes long distance runs, bergen marches, confidence and obstacle courses. The Q Course Phase I lasts five weeks and includes patrolling, close combat, evasion, insertion, survival and land navigation which are tested over 12 consecutive nights in the field.

That completes selection, but the would-be Green Beret has Q Course Phases II and III to go. Phase II lasts five weeks and includes individual specialities like weapons handling, explosives and demolitions, communications and first aid. Phase III, over four weeks, covers unconventional warfare and mission planning. It all ends with Exercise Robin Sage, a test exercise simulating operations in an insurgency.

The qualified Green Beret will continue with Advanced Training which includes regional orientation with a Special Forces group and advanced training at Fort Bragg, including sniping, High Altitude Low Opening (HALO) and High Altitude High Opening (HAHO) parachuting, underwater swimming, and operations and intelligence. Having gone through all these tests and collected new skills, Green Berets during the Vietnam War called their much coveted shoulder patch "The Saigon Electrical Works" – it is an arrowhead shape with a Commando

UH1 helicopters come into land in a jungle clearing. Universally known as the Huey it was the work horse in Vietnam.

knife and three lightning flashes superimposed. On their green berets soldiers sport the metal badge with the motto 'De Oppresso Liber' ('To liberate the oppressed') while officers wear their rank. Coloured backings to the beret badge show where the unit is based.

After Vietnam, US Army Special Forces, like the whole US Army, went through a period of self-critical reorganisation. They were employed in Op Urgent Fury in Grenada in 1983 and in Panama in Op Just

197

Cause, where prior to H-Hour they infiltrated key facilities around Panama City. On the Pacora Bridge a team prevented a Panamanian armoured task force from crossing and joining the fight by using Swedish AT-4 anti-tank weapons. As Panamanian pressure built up they called in C-130 Spectre Gunships to assist in holding the bridge.

In the Gulf Special Forces were employed in long range reconnaissance and intelligence gathering. One of their missions was to build up a picture of the deployment and strength of the Iraqi Republican Guard. Some teams inserted by helicopter found that it was impossible to dig hides in the rocky terrain, and were extracted. Other teams, dropped closer to the Euphrates, were able to dig into the agricultural land. However the area was full of farmers and civilians and some positions were compromised. In one action, helicopters and fixed wing aircraft flew deep into Iraq, and with cluster bombs exploding 'Danger Close' to the SF team, they were able to break contact and be lifted clear.

Special Forces with language skills were used to train Kuwaiti soldiers who had escaped after the Iraqi invasion, and acted as liaison officers between the Arab Coalition forces and the US Army. Psychological warfare operations, including leaflets, broadcasts and loudspeaker transmissions encouraged Iraqi troops to

A UH-60 Blackhawk helicopter landing in Grenada at sunrise. US Rangers suffered casualties when Blackhawks crashed during the operations, but during Desert Storm the UH-60 proved a very reliable troop lift helicopter.

defect and surrender, particularly when they were followed or preceded by heavy air attacks.

Delta Force

In 1977, following the success of the West German counter terrorist group GSG9, Colonel Charles 'Charging Charly' Beckwith convinced the US Army that there was a need for a counter-terrorist/hostage release organisation. Beckwith had been seconded to

199

A Huey lifts off from a dusty LZ. Troop carrying helicopters were known as (slicks) because they were smooth sided unlike the armed (hogs) which had machine guns and rockets.

22 SAS in 1963 and was impressed by the training and selection for the Regiment. The US Army group that was formed drew many of its features from 22 SAS and received the title Operational Detachment Delta. It is known as Delta Force or just Delta.

The force is about 400 strong, composed of two squadrons with a headquarters. The squadrons are broken down into four-man teams in which each member has a primary and secondary skill. Volunteers

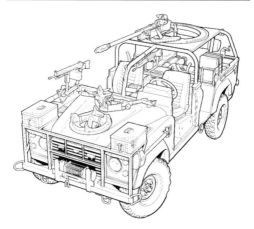

A line drawing of the SOV showing weapons and equipment stowage. A 30mm cannon is mounted on the roll bar frame while Heckler and Koch G3 rifles and the base plate and bipod of an 81mm mortar are attached to the bonnet.

are carefully screened by both officers and NCOs from Delta as well as psychologists to ensure that they are stable, but also capable of fast, almost reflex action. Fitness is important: as well as completing timed and speed and endurance marches, volunteers must

The helicopters in position on the flight deck of the USS Nimitz prior to the first leg of Eagle Claw which ended in disaster at the Desert One airstrip.

complete an inverted crawl over 40 yards in 25 seconds, swim 110 yards fully clothed and in boots, complete 37 sit-ups and 33 press-ups each in less than one minute. Weapons skills involve accurate, safe speed shooting with 100 per cent scores with a variety of weapons at 600 yards and 90 per cent at 1,000 yards.

Delta has a 'killing house' indoor close quarter battle (CQB) range like 22 SAS. It is known as 'the house of horrors' and is larger than the range at Hereford. There are four rooms, one of which represents an aircraft interior.

Delta personnel learn a number of standard skills like patrolling, intelligence gathering and long range secure communication, but also include vehicle theft,

RH-53 helicopters are readied on the morning of Operation Eagle Claw the abortive Delta Force hostage rescue mission in Iran in April 1980.

aircraft refuelling and hostage reassurance.

Delta has been used in Grenada, Panama and the Gulf. Its operational debut was the tragic Op Eagle Claw, the attempt to rescue the US Embassy staff held hostage in Tehran in 1980.

US Navy SEALS

US Naval SEALS – Sea-Air-Land units – have their origin in the naval frogmen of World War II and are the most highly trained of the American Special

Forces. They were created on 1 January 1962 under the direct orders of President JF Kennedy.

Trainees undergo a tough 23-week course at the Basic SEAL Training Department of the Naval Amphibious School, Coronado, which has a 55 per cent failure rate. They must already have qualified in a speciality like communications, must pass a tough diving medical and have to produce high scores on physical and mental aptitude tests. The first four weeks of the course consist of a two-week warm up followed by small boat handling, beach reconnaissance and long range patrolling. The fifth week, 'Hell Week', simulates operations with little sleep or food, and tests physical and mental stamina. Weeks 6 to 23 at San Clemente Island include long swims and free diving exercises, plus underwater and land demolitions.

Entry and exits from submarines are practised and the training ends with several small boat and swimming exercises including a five-mile marathon. On the static line parachute course students learn how to make wet drops into the sea with all their equipment. Advanced training at the Special Warfare Center and School, Fort Bragg, includes deep reconnaissance, operating mini-submarines and mine and bomb disposal. SEALs study a range of skills from languages to sniping, and make an effort to be

Members of the 7th Special Forces Group (Abn) photographed at Fort Bragg in 1980. Interestingly, one man has a British World War II vintage Sten gun.

qualified in two or more skills. The total selection and training period is up to a year, twice that of the Army Special Forces.

MACV Special Operations

Between 1966 and 1972 the US Joint Service High Command engaged in highly classified operations

205

with a force which peaked at 2,390 in 1971 and operated under the neutral title of Military Assistance Command Vietnam (MACV) Studies and Observation Group. It had five primary responsibilities: cross-border operations regularly conducted to disrupt the Viet Cong, Khmer Rouge, Pathet Lao and North Vietnamese Army (NVA) in their own territories; keeping track of imprisoned and missing Americans and conducting raids to assist and free them as part of the Escape and Evasion (E&E) mission for all captured US personnel and downed airmen; training and dispatching agents to North Vietnam to run resistance movement operations; 'Black' psychological operations such as establishing false (notional) NVA broadcasting stations inside North Vietnam; and 'Grey' psychological operations. MACV-SOG was also entrusted with specific tasks such as kidnapping, assassination, insertion of rigged mortar rounds into the enemy ammunition supply chain, and retrieval of sensitive documents or equipment lost or captured through enemy action.

To undertake this work the Americans, who were largely Special Forces, were assisted by over 8,000 highly trained indigenous troops. They were grouped as Spike Recon Teams (RT), Hatchet Forces and Search-Location-and-Annihilation-Mission Companies (SLAM). RTs consisted of three US

At the Flint Kaserne, Bad Tolz Germany on a Leadership and Team Building Training Exercise are supervised by Ranger Cadre from the United States in December 1985.

Special Forces soldiers and nine indigenous soldiers from the mountain minority tribes.

MACV-SOG had its own air force (the 90th Special Operations Wing) which consisted of a squadron of USAF 'Green Hornet' helicopters, a squadron of C-130 transports, a covert C-123 squadron flown by Nationalist Chinese Air Force crews, and the South Vietnamese 219th H-34 helicopter squadron. The US Navy provided SEALS, Vietnamese Underwater

A HMMWV or Humvee armed with a .50 Browning. The Humvee is larger than a Land Rover, but is a stable vehicle with a substantial payload which makes it ideal for long range patrols.

Demolition Teams (UDT) and fast patrol boats.

To run this type of operation, particularly as a covert one, required organisation as well as secrecy. The MACV-SOG Command and Control Central (CCC) was based at Kontum; CC North was at Da Nang, and CC South at Ban Me Thuot. All operated between 1967 and 1971. A training centre for Cambodian forces operated in various locations in Vietnam from 1970 to 1972. It ran an intensive 15 week programme which turned Cambodian recruits into combat-ready light infantrymen.

MACV-SOG was deactivated on 30 April 1972 and replaced by the Strategic Directorate Assistance Team 158 on 1 May 1972. This team was subsequently deactivated on 13 March 1973. Like the Private Armies of World War II, MACV-SOG had had its day.

Spetsnaz

During World War II the Soviet Army had used their parachute forces in small-scale operations, dropping five to eighty men to attack key points or assist Partisans. In one major attack in September 1943, the 7,000 men of the 5th Guards Parachute Brigade, 3rd Brigade and the 1st Brigade were dropped to support a Red Army attack at the Bukrin bridge-head. Among their number were medical staff who were exclusively female. By a tragic mischance their DZ was in an area through which the 10th Panzer Grenadier Division and the 19th Panzer Division were moving. The Germans drove into them and in a few days they were reduced to a force of 2,300 men, mostly from the 3rd and 5th Brigades. These survivors fought on as Partisans.

Grenada 1983: Cubans detained by men of the US 82nd Airborne. There were rumours that among the Cubans were members of the Soviet special forces, in fact they were construction workers.

The Soviet Army mounted no more airborne operations for the rest of the war. However, after the war the paratroop arm or Vozdushno-Desantnaya Voyska (VDV) became an elite but separate arm of the Soviet Government. The VDV was composed entirely of men from the western USSR. Most of them had qualified as parachutists during DOSAAF, their pre-conscription youth training, and were also

A spread of weapons captured in Grenada. Special forces are trained to handle foreign weapons and this collection is an interesting challenge including British and Eastern Bloc weapons.

reliable Party members. This made the VDV a superb instrument of Soviet government policy. Paratroopers operating as ground forces went into Czechoslovakia in Op Danube in August 1968 and spearheaded the occupation of Afghanistan in December 1979. In both countries the VDV provided the muscle backing up smaller scale but exactly targeted operations by the Soviet Special Forces or Voiska Spetsialnogo

211

Naznacheniya, better known as Spetsnaz.

Until the late 1950s special operations were the responsibility of the VDV, but then came the creation of the Spetsnaz organisations of the KGB (Komitet Gosudarstvennoi Bezopastnosti) and GRU (Glavnoye Razvedyvatelnoye Upravleniye). Interestingly it is reported that 90 per cent of the manpower for both organisations was drawn from conscripts. However, like the VDV, the highly centralised Soviet state could identify suitable men at conscription age. They would arrive proficient in a range of military skills from DOSAAF. Language skills and sports achievements would count in their favour. In effect a selection process had already taken place before the men arrived in the armed forces.

The KGB Spetsnaz comprised a small cadre of professionals assisted by several hundred support personnel and focused on social, economic and political targets at the highest level. KGB Spetsnaz operators were based in most major embassies, from which they undertook selected operations in great secrecy. Their duties included the grimly euphemistic 'mokrie dela' or 'wet jobs' – the assassination of important hostile figures and regional political leaders. During the Cold War the KGB Spetsnaz also used Bulgarian and East German proxies.

The existence of the military wing of Spetsnaz

Close combat skills taught in the Soviet Army included anti-tank tactics which drew on experience from the 'Great Patriotic War', as they call World War II.

attached to the Second Directorate of the GRU was already known in the West when it was admitted by the Soviet Union as the Cold War drew to a close. The basic Spetsnaz unit was the Special Operations Brigade (Brigada osobovo naznacheniya) which consists of three or four airborne battalions. There were 16 brigades allotted one per group-of-forces (military districts). In East Germany eight brigade strength groups – the Group of Soviet Forces in Germany (GSFG) – were based at Neuruppen. In a war in Europe they would have targeted NATOs political direction by neutralising key personnel and

213

Soviet special forces clear a building on a training area, which to give added realism has been set alight.

destroying its command, control and communications. NATOs strategic and tactical nuclear capability was a key target, since its destruction would prevent any effective counter-strike being launched when the war went nuclear, as Soviet planners intended it should. Target dossiers had been prepared on airfields, naval bases and air defence installations. In Afghanistan the GRU Spetsnaz became a potent anti-guerrilla force.

A Mi8 HIP helicopter drops a Soviet marine reconnaissance patrol on a beach during operation 'Comrades in Arms' in East Germany in 1980.

Spetsnaz in Czechoslovakia

In August 1968 300,000 to 400,000 Warsaw Pact and Soviet troops were used to suppress the democracy movement in Czechoslovakia known as the 'Prague Spring'. Spetsnaz troops played an important part. When an unscheduled Aeroflot aircraft landed at Prague's Ruzyne Airport late at night on 19 August, taxied and parked at the end of the runway, the airport authorities were not unduly worried. An hour later a second aircraft landed and its young, fit male passengers cleared customs and made their way into

215

Soviet paratroops await to board their Antonov An-12 transport: the USSR maintained six airborne divisions.

town. Two hours later the 'passengers' were back, fully armed, to take control of the airport.

With the airport secure, two more aircraft carrying uniformed Spetsnaz arrived. They were rapidly followed by further flights which included men of the 103rd Guards Airborne Division. Within two hours the airport was secure and the Spetsnaz and Airborne forces were on the road to Prague. By dawn they had secured the Presidential Palace, radio and television studios and transmitter, all the main stations and bridges over the Vltava.

In Exercise West 81 paratroops fire a 23mm ZU-23. This light anti-aircraft gun has been widely used in a ground role in conflicts world wide.

Czechoslovakia's experiment in limited democracy – 'Socialism with a human face' – was snuffed out as part of the Soviet policy of 'normalization' propounded by First Secretary Leonid Brezhnev, which became known as the 'Brezhnev Doctrine'. It had cost a total of 70 dead and 1,000 wounded –

Following page: Senior Warrant Officer A Turkov demonstrates his close combat skills on a range in the USSR in 1990. Training standards have slipped since the end of the Soviet Union.

The strain shows on the faces of men on a cross country march. The man on the right is armed with the RPG-16D anti-tank weapon, while the radio operator has a R-126 radio.

Previous page: An AK74 armed soldier clears a combined range and assault course in the USSR.

seen as an acceptable price for keeping Czechoslovakia a reliable member of the Warsaw Pact.

Invasion of Afghanistan

Almost ten years later Spetsnaz and airborne forces were deployed as an instrument of Soviet policy in Afghanistan. A Communist coup in April 1978

220

Unarmed combat training in a well equipped gym for men of a commando unit of the Kantemirovskaya Armoured Division in January 1989.

produced a general uprising against the government of the Democratic Government of Afghanistan (DRA). The Soviet Union poured in aid advisers and assistance for 18 months. They then decided that, since the government of Hafizullah Amin – who had eliminated his only rival for power, Nur Mohammed Taraki – was still losing the war, it was time to change it. Between 8 and 10 December, two weeks before the air and land invasion, Spetsnaz troops with an airborne regiment moved into Bagram to the north of

221

Kabul and secured the tactically important Salang Highway and tunnel. Between 10 and 24 December, Spetsnaz troops and an airborne battalion moved to Kabul International Airport which is less than 3 kilometres from the capital. Between 24 and 27 December, men from the 105th Guards Airborne Division with Spetsnaz support landed and secured Kabul airport and the Afghan Air Force bases at Bagram, Shindland, and Kandahar.

During the night of the 27th, the paratroopers went into action. They arrested the Afghan government while Spetsnaz teams demolished the central military communications centre, and captured the still functioning Ministry of the Interior, the Kabul radio station and other key points. Two regular Spetsnaz companies, with KGB assistance and backed by an airborne regiment, attacked President Amin's palace at Darulaman with the intention of arresting him. His security guards resisted and the action cost the Soviet forces 25 dead, one of whom was a KGB Colonel named Balashika who was killed in the crossfire. Whether Amin and his family committed suicide or became a 'wet job' is not known, but they died violently. His government was replaced by one led by Babrak Karmal, a Soviet puppet, and the Brezhnev Doctrine appeared to have worked.

The war in Afghanistan had only just begun for the

In one piece camouflaged coveralls soviet
reconnaissance troops are briefed prior to a training
exercise.

Soviet Army. Up to 1983 Spetsnaz conscript troops defended their barracks and major installations. In 1983 they begun to be used in offensive operations. Groups which varied in strength from scout teams to full battalions were lifted by Mi-4 Hound helicopters, carried by trucks, or moved in on foot. They ambushed the supply routes from Pakistan, mined choke-points like fords, directed air strikes, and attacked villages friendly to the Mujihadeen.

Spetsnaz troops wore either standard Soviet Airborne uniforms or even those of the DRA, since the Mujihadeen knew that the DRA were a soft target and unlikely to fight hard.

In 1988 First Secretary Mikhail Gorbachev announced that the Soviet Union would pull out from Afghanistan and by 15 February 1989 the last soldier had withdrawn. By 1991 the old Soviet Union was collapsing and with it the status and funding of the Armed Forces. The poor performance of the Russian Army in the invasion of the breakaway state of Chechnya in December 1995 showed that the training and motivation of the forces had reached a new low.

The disastrous attempt to release 300 hostages held by about 150 Chechens in the village of Pervomaiskoye, which reportedly was undertaken by men of a Special Forces group called the Alpha

The compact AKSU-74 which was first used in Afghanistan in 1982 is favoured by Russian special forces.

Commando, was drawn out over ten days. The village was bombarded by BM21 'Grad' 122mm rocket launchers and Mi-24D attack helicopters. When finally the Russian forces entered the ruins, 50 Chechen rebels were dead, but 25 had escaped with their leader Salman Raduyev and over a dozen Russian policemen who were captured during the siege.

Israeli Special Forces

If the Russian performance at Pervomaiskoye is a grim example of how not to undertake a rescue operation, the Israeli operation in 1976 to release hostages held by a group of terrorists at Entebbe, in Uganda, is a model of how these operations should be conducted. The terrorists were two men from the Popular Front for the Liberation of Palestine (PFLP), and a man and woman from the German Baader-Meinhof gang. The PFLP – headed by Dr George Habash, known by his followers as al-Hakim 'the wise one' – was one of a dozen Middle East terrorist organisations that launched attacks in Europe in the 1970s and 80s in an attempt to harm Israel and its allies.

At 0900hrs on 27 June 1976, an Air France A-300

The Israeli UZI submachine gun is a reliable and robust weapon which is used by both military and special forces.

An Israeli Air Force C130 Hercules lands after the Entebbe operation on July 4, 1976.

In training exercises, prior to the rescue operation, the paratroopers established how quickly they could land at Entebbe and exit their C130s with their vehicles.

Airbus with 253 passengers took off from Tel Aviv. At 1210hrs, shortly after leaving Athens airport, it was hijacked and ordered to be flown to Benghazi. It landed there and after six-and-a-half hours on the ground took off again and flew south to land at Entebbe at about 0315hrs on 28 June. Here President Idi Amin gave the terrorists a tacit agreement that he would not interfere and would even offer some help, allowing nine more PFLP terrorists to join the group.

The hostages were moved from the aircraft to the

The old airport terminal at Entebbe, Uganda.

old airport terminal where the building was guarded by Ugandan soldiers. The hijackers demanded the release of a number of Palestinians held in jails in Europe and said that if their demands were not met, they would start to kill their hostages from 1200hrs on 1 July.

Playing for time, the Israeli Prime Minister Yitzhak Rabin said that they were willing to consider the release of prisoners, but that negotiations would take time. The hijackers extended the deadline and released non-Israeli hostages, though the captain of the aircraft elected to remain with his passengers. The

229

released passengers and crew were debriefed and helped Mossad, the Israeli intelligence service, build up a more detailed picture. The Israelis now knew where in the building the 89 Jewish hostages were being held.

The Israelis were now in a better position to launch a rescue operation. The major problem was that Lockheed C130 transport aircraft would not have sufficient fuel to make a return flight from Uganda to Israel. Behind the scenes negotiating secured clearance for the rescue flight to land at Nairobi airport to refuel. In a rehearsal attack on a scale model of the airport terminal on 3 July the rescuers, commanded by Brigadier Dan Shomron, took 55 minutes – the time allocated in the plan. At 1600hrs, two hours after the full Israeli cabinet had given its assent to the rescue operation, six aircraft took off.

Four were C130s which would carry the hostages and their rescuers, one was a Boeing 707 fitted out as a flying hospital which went straight to Nairobi airport, while a Boeing 707 command and control aircraft provided the radio link to Nairobi. They flew down the Red Sea, swung inland along the Sudan/Ethiopian border and then into Ugandan air space. Their transit was not picked up by Saudi Arabian radar nor by the Ugandans.

The first C130 landed close to the control tower

A variation on a theme, an Israeli M151 362kg vehicle in Lebanon with a MAG in the passenger's seat and one in the back.

and its load of paratroopers quickly secured it and ensured that landing lights would not be switched off. A fourth C130 taxied to the control tower as the other two went for the old terminal. The paratroopers cut down twenty startled Ugandan soldiers and raced into the building.

The two German terrorists Wilfried Boese and Gabriele Tiedemann, who were more alert than their PFLP comrades, were the first to die. The paratroops

231

shouted for the hostages to stay down, but tragically three were killed in the crossfire. The PFLP terrorists who were upstairs were killed by the paratroops.

Two other groups of paratroops were moving rapidly through the airport. One used explosive charges to attack the six Ugandan Air Force MiG-15, MiG-17 and MiG-21 fighters based at Entebbe. This removed a potential threat to the force when it took off, but also served as a spectacular diversion. A third moved to secure the perimeter against a Ugandan Army counter-attack.

Some of the hostages ran to the aircraft, while others were ferried in jeeps that had been flown in. Three hostages had been killed (and Mrs Dora Bloch who had been taken to a hospital was subsequently murdered by Ugandan troops), while the paratroops had only suffered three men wounded. As the perimeter security group was called in, it looked as if the operation would be a remarkable success. Tragically, a Ugandan soldier on the roof of the old terminal fired at the 30-year-old Lt Col Jonathan Netanyahu, who had led the hostage rescue group, fatally wounding him.

The Israeli force had spent 44 minutes on the ground – 11 minutes less than their rehearsal time. The last aircraft took off at 0054hrs, and they reached Nairobi at 0239hrs. Here ten wounded were transferred to the Boeing 707 hospital aircraft. After refuelling they took off for Israel between 0338 and 0408hrs.

The success at Entebbe was down to a combination of excellent training, good intelligence, clear missions and aggressive but intelligent leadership. The failure at Pervomaiskaya reflected the unreliable leadership of Boris Yeltsin and the low esteem and self-esteem of the Russian armed forces, as well as poor intelligence and a crude firepower overkill.

French Special Forces

The post war French Army was pitched into conflicts almost immediately. In Indo-China it fought a war from 1946 to 1954 against the Communist/ Nationalist Viet Minh. Though for many soldiers much of this involved patrolling and guarding key points against sabotage, elite French forces were committed to deep penetration actions against the Viet Minh.

Men from the 1st and 2nd Battalions of the Foreign Legion Parachutists (BEP) and the 1st, 2nd, 3rd, 5th, 6th and 8th Battalions of the Colonial Paratroops (BPC) were the spearhead for raids against Viet Minh logistics dumps. In November 1952 dumps in the area of Phu Doan were attacked by a combined airborne and armoured operation. It yielded 34 mortars, 30 anti-tank rockets, 40 machine

guns, 250 rifles, and two 57 mm recoilless guns. In
addition, factories and food dumps were destroyed
and, to the considerable interest of the French, a
Russian Molotova truck was captured.

At the caves at Lang Son and Loc Binh in the
following year the paratroops were committed to a
more hazardous operation close to the Chinese
border. Operation Hirondelle (Swallow) was kept a
close secret and security paid off, the paratroops from
the 6th and 8th BPC and 2 BEP captured so much
food fuel, vehicles, weapons and ammunition that
they used fire and 800 kg of explosives to destroy it.
The return journey overland was a 48 hour speed
march in tropical heat. The Viet Minh caught up
with the paratroops moments too late as they were
boarding trucks at Dinh Lap and opened ineffective
fire at long range. The operation which had dealt a
very effective blow to the Viet Minh logistic chain
had cost the French one dead, one missing, three dead
from exhaustion and 21 wounded who were
evacuated by helicopter. At this stage in the war in
Indo China helicopters were a rare resource, used only
for casualty evacuation. Later the French would make
extensive use of them in Algeria in operations which
would be a small scale model for US Army airmobile
operations in Viet Nam in the 1960s and 70s.

In 1953 the French opted to fight a conventional

battle against the Viet Minh at Dien Bien Phu, a valley in north east Viet Nam when they parachuted forces into what was meant to become an land and air base deep inside Viet Minh controlled territory. It would be the final battle of the war in Indo China as the Viet Minh surrounded the base and after a prolonged siege finally defeated the French. Men, ammunition and supplies had to be parachuted in after dark as the siege tightened. On the night of May 3 a company of the 1st BCP jumped in to reinforce the besieged French position. It was commanded by Lt Marcel Edme an officer who had served with the French squadron of the SAS in World War II and sported a British Parachute Regiment maroon beret.

In Algeria between 1954 and 1962 the French fought both a counter-terrorist and guerrilla war. In the city of Algiers a war against the National Liberation Front (FLN) saw the use of informers and counter gangs by Colonel Yves Godard as well as cordon and search and interrogation. In the city the FLN used bombs and assassinations as well as intimidation to attack the European parts of Algiers as well as controlling the Arab quarter of the Casbah to the north. Paratroopers who had been fighting against FLN units in the Aures mountains were brought into the city and prosecuted the campaign rigorously.

Later under Air Force General Maurice Challe a
series of operations were launched in 1959 which
rolled the FLN back towards the Tunisian border. The
first was launched at Saida in the bitter February of
that year and then in the Quarseis Mountains Op
Courroie ran through April. Meanwhile in the
mountains of the Great Kabylia and the Hodna,
operation Jumelles ran from July to October and
netted nearly 4,000 FLN prisoners. Finally, in
November that year, operations were undertaken near
Constantine. The final phase in General Challe's
campaign was to be Operation Trident launched in
1960 in the Aures. The French armed forces,
supported by local Algerian Arab troops called harkis
had won the military campaign.

After its experience in Viet Nam the French Army
had developed concepts of revolutionary warfare
which were similar in character to the "hearts and
minds" operations of the SAS. In Viet Nam small
detachments of French soldiers had lived in villages to
provide security and assistance to these communities;
in Algeria the Army launched education and health
programmes. One young officer detached to a remote
mountain community startled his headquarters when
he requested a consignment of cosmetics and
stockings, he explained that he wanted to wean the
Arab women away from the strictures of Islam

towards French and European attitudes, and one way was to persuade them to adopt European clothing and styles.

At the close of the war France was faced by a different terrorist threat, from European Algerians who were not prepared to see Algeria become an independent Arab state. The Secret Army Organisation or OAS was a threat to Metropolitan France as well as Algeria and led to the formation of covert counter-terrorist teams. It had been formed in part by Col Godard following an attempted coup d'etat in April 1961 by Generals Edmond Jouhaud, Raoul Salan, Maurice Challe and Henri Zeller. In the aftermath of the coup the 1st Foreign Legion Parachute Regiment (1 REP) was disbanded and many para officers throughout the Army were posted abroad or found their careers restricted.

The OAS contained many men with military experience and access to weapons and explosives and to combat them the French government formed a secret organisation which was nicknamed barbouzes - false beards. he barbouzes were recruited on a haphazard basis and inadequately trained. The OAS penetrated their operations and in March 1962 blew up their headquarters in the Hotel Rajah. There were several attempts by the OAS to kill President Charles de Gaulle, who had accepted that despite the fact that the French Army had won the military campaign in Algeria, France had lost the political battle, and the long term cost to France to maintain forces in Algeria was too great to justify the returns.

The French Army after Algeria went through a traumatic period of re-adjustment. However it still retained an interest in its colonies and former colonies and was prepared to commit soldiers or Gendarmes to stabilise governments. In February 1976 men of the 2nd Coy 2 REP supported by armoured cars of the 13th Foreign Legion Half Brigade (13 DBLE) and a Gendarmerie unit, took part in a hostage rescue operation in Djibouti. A school bus was hijacked by Somalian terrorists and driven to the Somali border at Loyoda. Apart from the kidnappers the legionnaires faced covering fire from Somali troops on the border. In the operation two children were killed and five wounded and a Legion officer and two adults in the bus were hurt. Seven terrorists died as well as an unknown number of Somali troops whose positions had been shot up by 90 mm and machine gun fire from the 13 DBLE.

In May 1978 men of the 2 REP made an epic drop over the copper and uranium mining town of Kolwezi in Zaire's Shaba province. The town and 2,300 European and Asian mining staff with their families had been seized by Katangese rebels of the "Congolese

Men of 2 REP exit from a C130 at Kolwezi during the second lift. The man in the centre has a 7.62 mm AA52 general purpose machine gun.

National Liberation Front" (FNLC) who had crossed from Angola. Initially the self-styled "Tigers" looted the town and killed Zairean inhabitants, but then they begun beat, rape, torture and kill the Europeans. Some were "tried" in front of "courts" for "collaboration" with President Mobuto's government. The Zairean Army was unable to intervene and even Belgium, the former colonial power said that it could

only provide humanitarian aid. Mobuto appealed to
the French President Giscard d'Estaing and early on
the morning of May 17 a signal was sent to Calvi,
Corsica warning Lt Col Erulin that his regiment 2
REP was on six hours' notice to move.

The operation code named "Leopard" was a superb
example of what well trained and experienced troops
can achieve. By 20.00 on the 17th the regiment had
been assembled and by 01.30 on the 18th the
movement order had arrived. At 08.00 the bulk of 2
REP were at Corsica's Solenzara airport. The tactical
HQ, four rifle companies, and the mortar and
reconnaissance platoons - 650 men, flew 6,000 km to
Kinshasa in Zaire aboard French DC-8s. The second
echelon with the regiment's vehicles, would fly in later
to Lubumbashi, Shaba province's capital aboard
USAF C-5 and C-141 transports.

By 23.30 on the 18th Erulin and his HQ staff were
working to put together an operational battalion
jump which though it would be undertaken with a
minimum of support and equipment could expect to
have to be self sufficient for at least three days. Enemy
numbers and equipment were unknown as was the
area identified as a DZ.

The Legion paras had four USAF C-130s and one
C-160 and unfamiliar US T-10 parachutes. Weapons
bundles and equipment were rigged to the harness

240

with tape and parachute cord. In the event the big T-10s saved many men from injury as they gave a slower descent and consequent softer landing on the rock hard African soil. Despite loading restrictions, the 2 REP planners packed 80 men aboard C-130 designed for 66 and in this way 405 legionnaires were able to take off at 11.30 on the 19th. It took four hours to reach the DZ.

The drop on DZ Alpha an area of elephant grass and termite hills at the north east corner of the Old Town was scattered but met little opposition. While the 3rd Coy held the bridge leading from the New Town to the east, the 1st headed towards the Jean XXIII school a kilometre away and the 2nd headed to the hospital and Gecamines complex 2.5 km away. Both companies had running fire fights with the FNLC in the scrub and back alleys. The sight of corpses, black and white, gave the operation added impetus. By the end of the day all the objectives had been secured, an attack from the New Town by three FNLC armoured cars had been beaten off with loss and the first hostages , hysterical with relief, had been released from the Jean XXIII school.

On the following day the Mortar and Recce Platoon with 4th Coy parachuted in and on the 20th. The 1st and 2nd Coys cleared the south and west quarters of the Old Town and went to the support of 4 Coy which was involved in a fierce fire fight in the northern Metal-Shaba suburb. The 3rd Coy pushed south to the Manika estate. In his HQ at the bloodstained and battered Impala Hotel Col Erulin began to organise the hostage evacuation flights.

On the 21st the regiment's vehicles arrived from Lubumbashi and for the next week the 2 REP patrolled over a 300 kilometre radius. There were sharp clashes at Kapata and Luilu. On the 28th the regiment pulled out for Lubumbashi and by June 4 they were back in Corsica. Operation Leopard had cost them five dead and 25 wounded. They had killed about 250 FNLC and captured 163. They had knocked out two armoured cars and captured four recoilless riffles, 15 mortars, 21 rocket launchers, ten machine guns, and 275 assorted small arms. Most importantly they had saved 2,000 civilians from what would have been horrible deaths.

Within the French Army the1 RPIMA or 1st Paratroop Marine Infantry continues the traditions of the World War II French SAS squadron. It is composed three rifle companies and a training company. In Operation Manta in 1983 it was deployed to Chad. The central African state had been split by civil war between elements of the Toubou tribe in which Libya, its northern neighbour, had begun meddling and attempting to annex territory. To the north were men

A Chadian vehicle fitted out with a French Chatellerault M1924/29 LMG and Soviet ZU-23 23mm anti-aircraft gun.

under Goukouni Oueddei with his Libyan patron Colonel Ghadafi, while to the south was Hissene Habre. Ghadafi's interest in the country was explained by the existence of uranium deposits in the north. France, with discreet support from the United States, backed Habre. The country was wracked by four civil wars, which climaxed in February 1986. It began when Oueddei decided to make peace with Habre, but was shot and wounded "while resisting arrest" in Tripoli. The northern Toubou changed sides and invited Habre to come to their rescue.

French weapons, training and advisors combined with a cavalry-style panache of the Chadians produced a series of "David and Goliath" victories. In many ways the tactics were similar to those of the SAS in North Africa in World War II. Mobility and fire power were traded off against protection. The Chadian forces moved north in open topped Toyota 4 x 4 vehicles fitted with Milan anti-tank missiles and .50 machine guns and AML 90 armoured cars. The Milan is a man portable missile with an effective range of 2,000 meters. The AML 90 is a compact 4 x 4 vehicle with a crew of three and a maximum road speed of 90 kph.

On January 2, 1987 Habre's forces took Fada a cross-roads in the desert and captured dozens of Soviet made T-55 tanks and six Italian anti-aircraft guns. On March 19 a Libyan armoured column set out from Wadi Doum an air base in north-central Chad, intent on recapturing Fada. It was ambushed and destroyed and when a second rescue column set out from Faya-Largeau it too was ambushed and destroyed. In the two battles over 800 Libyans were killed by Chadian forces. Habres forces moved on to capture Wadi Doum on March 21 and on the 27th Faya-Largeau.

The Chadians killed 1,200 Libyans at Faya and took an immense amount of booty including Tupolev

At the moment of firing a Milan missile tube is ejected to the rear as the missile is launched off a commercial truck in Chad in 1986

bombers, MiG-21s, helicopters, three complete batteries of SAM 13s and supporting radar and over 100 tanks. The value of this weapons was put at between $500 million and $1 billion.

By the end of March, Chad had claimed to have killed 3,603 Libyans and captured 1165 for a loss of 35 Chadians. Many of these "Libyans" turned out to be mercenaries including Sudanese who had no idea

245

where they were. There were also 1,700 Druse militia men from Lebanon who had been hired out by their leader Walid Jumblatt at a monthly rate of $500 to $2,300 per man.

In August Habre's men drove the Libyans out of the Aozou strip on the Libya /Chad border but without French air support they were vulnerable to counter attack. The Libyans re-took Aozou and even flew journalists out to the desert to prove it. Habre avenged this defeat by sending a column over 100 km into Libya and destroying the Libyan air base at Matan as-Sarra. In the raid the Chadians lost 65 men but claimed to have killed 1,700 Libyans and taken 312 prisoners which included East German and Yugoslav advisors and technicians.

In a proxy war funded partly by the United States, backed by French weapons, logistics and advisors the Chadians had inflicted a defeat on the Libyans which had cost them 7,500 men killed or one tenth of the army as well as $1.5 billion in equipment captured or destroyed.

In 1995-96 French forces were 12 countries, and were contributing to peace-keeping operations in 13 countries. The French now have a 42,500 strong Rapid Reaction Force (FAR) which includes airborne and air mobile forces.

In the Gendarmerie Nationale the Government has

Men of the 1 RPIMA with a Hotchkiss Jeep in the harsh sunlight of Chad

a valuable "third force" which is more powerful than a conventional police force with 41 helicopters, 340 armoured wheeled vehicles and 278 81mm mortars as well as 25 small river craft, but which is not part of the armed forces. The 93,400 men and women enjoy a status similar to the Army and its officers attend staff courses with the Army. It was therefore the obvious basis for a counter-terrorist and hostage rescue force.

The Groupe d'Intervention de Gendarmerei

Nationale or GIGN enjoys something of celebrity status in France, which has always been fascinated by elites. The 50 men of GIGN have been in action against Algerian terrorists who hijacked an airliner to Marseilles in 1985 and against an individual kidnapper who seized children in a Paris primary school. In joint exercises with the Kent Constabulary, and SAS they have examined the options open in a terrorist hijack of a Eurostar train in the Channel Tunnel.

The order of battle of the French Army includes 31,000 Fusiliers Marin in 15 regiments including Regiments Parachutist d'Infanterie de Marine or RPIMA. However the French Navy have their own Marines, this is an elite force of 3,900 men who wear a green beret with a distinctive shield shaped badge which reflects their origins in World War II showing a fishing boat used in cross Channel raids, the cross of Lorraine and a FS Commando knife.

Within the Marines is GROUFUMACO or Groupement des Fusiliers-Marins Commando some 400 Commandos in three assault groups designated Jaubert. Penfentenyo, Trepel with the support commando Montfort with the Hubert attack swimmer unit based at Toulon. There is also a reserve commando Francoise. Their roles include unconventional warfare tasked directly by the national

The captain of the hijacked Air France A-300 Airbus and his passengers leave the C130 at the end of one of the most successful hostage release operations this century.

command authorities if so required. They can be used in support of French Navy operations, and tasked with supporting the operations of 9th Marine Division in the force protection role, although it is not subordinated to this division's headquarters. The Hubert swimmers conduct beach reconnaissance for amphibious operations and attack shipping using limpet mines. A limpet mine was used by French intelligence to attack the Greenpeace ship Rainbow

Warrior which had been monitoring nuclear tests while it was anchored in Auckland harbour.

Within the 10 parachute regiments which make up the French 11th Parachute Division (DP) are commando teams with a designation which sounds a little unusual to British or American ears. They are CRAP or Commandos de Recherche et d'Action en Profondeur. There are two CRAPs within a regiment, one working for the HQ Company (CCS) and the other for the Reconnaissance and Support Company (CEA). They are tasked with deep penetration operations including intelligence and direct action. Skills include High Altitude Low Opening (HALO) from 6,000 meters and High Altitude High Opening (HAHO) parachuting, SCUBA operations with submarines and Zodiac inflatables navigation, demolitions and secure signals. Operating deep inside hostile territory CRAPs are self-sufficient and so men carry loads of up to 65 kilograms. In large scale conventional jumps they serve as path finders.

The selection process for CRAPs is classified, but an indication of its severity can be gauged by the training and selection for the 2 REP. Recruits for the Foreign Legion have a three month course which begins with 30 days of drill, running, inspections and marches with full kit. These begin 10 km in week one, 15 km in week two, 20 km in week three and a gruelling 60

A French Air Force Jaguar attack aircraft lifts off from a base in Saudi Arabia during the Gulf War. Jaguars were used for close support and airfield denial in Chad.

km in the final week. In the second month recruits continue with drill and forced marches and start weapons training. There is a 500 meter assault course which must be completed in under five minutes. In the third month recruits undertake mountain and winter warfare training. This includes a 200 km mountain march in four days in full kit. After completing his training the Legionnaire receives his white kepi. To join the 2 REP the candidate must pass the para-commando course which includes close-quarter battle training, endurance marches, signals, navigation, demolitions, Zodiac operations, jungle and mountain training.

A French Panhard ERC 90 F4 Sagaie armoured car fitted with a GIAT TS90 turret and 90mm gun during operations in the Gulf in 1991.

Interestingly there are CRAPs within the para engineers of the 17th RGP and the gunners of the 35th RAP. The CRAP of the 2nd Foreign Legion Parachute Regiment (REP) was deployed in deep penetration operations during the Gulf War of 1990-91. CRAPs do not have obvious distinctive insignia except a breast badge five stars within an arc and the letters CRAP. The CRAP of the 1st RPIMA and 13th Regiment Dragons Parachutists (RDP) are an elite, within an elite since both the 1 RPIMA and 13 RDP are SF rolled.

Plans for the French Army in the 21st Century include making it an all volunteer force, at the moment out of 241,400 some 136,800 are conscripts serving a year and 8,600 are women in clerical and support roles. It is planned to reduce its size and make it a more flexible instrument of government policy, capable of rapid deployment overseas with experienced well trained troops. For this work the ability of SF to launch small scale but effective operations will be critical. The challenge for the French, as with every Army is to identify and select the sort of men who can fulfil these roles. The conscript pool may have been misused in the past but it will be missed since it provides a useful source of intelligent recruits.

Special Forces in the 21st century

Some countries have a 'Third Force' – a Gendarmerie which has a role between that of the Police and the Army and which is therefore, like the 50 men of the French GIGN, the ideal force for hostage release and counter terrorism. However, many do not. The existence of regional police forces in Germany meant that the Federal hostage release and anti-terrorist force GSG9 had to be based on the Border Police. Many national Police federations would rather have the hostage release and counter terrorist role conducted

by an outside force, so there is certainly one job
guaranteed for Army Special Forces.

Peace-keeping or peace-making in the 21st Century
will ensure that soldiers continue to be sent to hostile
and potentially lethal environments. Special Forces
will find themselves working in close protection roles
as body-guards for VIPs and senior officers, and at the
other end of the spectrum as forward air controllers
designating targets for Laser Guided Bombs (LGBs).
The 1,000lb LGB, accurately delivered, is an

*Wearing snow shoes and pulling a sled men of Canada's
Special Service Force cradle their 7.62mm SLRs.
Canada has now adopted the 5.56mm M16A2 rifle.*

The remarkable accuracy of a GBU-100 Laser Guided Bomb (LGB) is demonstrated as it hits the cab of a target vehicle. LGBs were first used in the closing phases of the Vietnam war.

economical and effective show of force – iron or 'dumb' bombs scattered across the country make for a bad press or a propaganda victory.

Possibly the only role in which special forces are unlikely to find employment in the forseeable future is working with guerrilla forces in a low-intensity war against a major power. They may however be fighting guerrilla wars driven by drugs, religion or nationalism well into the 21st Century.

255

Other titles in the Collins/Jane's Gems series will include:

Aircraft of World War II

A handy guide to the warplanes of World War II from the Battle of Britain to the airwar against Japan. Includes over 100 warplanes from all major air forces, with technical data and photographs. A historical introduction explains how the biplanes of the 1930s evolved into fast monoplane fighters and eventually jets.

Modern tanks

A complete guide to the tank forces of the 1990s, featuring over 100 combat vehicles with photographs and technical specifications. An introductory section reveals the latest developments in tank technology and explains how tanks are adapting to the new challenges of the modern battlefield. From veterans like the T-55 to the M1 Abrams and the XM-8, this includes every main battle tank produced since World War II.

Combat aircraft

A concise guide to military aircraft today, from the ultra-modern F-117 Nighthawk, better known as the 'Stealth' bomber to the veteran warplanes like the Boeing B-52 and McDonnell Douglas F-4 Phantom. An introductory section reveals the latest developments in military aircraft and how designs are changing now the Cold War is over.